FILMMAKERS
On
FILMMAKING

Also Available from J. P. Tarcher, Inc.

FILMMAKERS ON FILMMAKING, Volume 2
edited by Joseph McBride
> Norman Lear, Studio Executive
> Joseph E. Levine, Producer
> Jean Renoir, Director
> Robert Towne, Screenwriter
> Charlton Heston, Actor
> Bette Davis, Actress
> John A. Alonzo, Cinematographer
> Jerry Goldsmith, Composer
> Harry Horner, Production Designer
> Edith Head, Costume Designer
> Joyce Selznick, Casting Director
> Stan Brakhage, Independent Filmmaker

Other Books by Joseph McBride

John Huston (editor)
Frank Capra (editor)
Hawks on Hawks
Astaire (editor)
High & Inside: The Complete Guide to Baseball Slang
Orson Welles: Actor and Director
Kirk Douglas
John Ford (with Michael Wilmington)
Focus on Howard Hawks (editor)
Orson Welles
Persistence of Vision (editor)

FILMMAKERS *On* FILMMAKING

The American Film Institute
Seminars on Motion Pictures and Television

Edited by Joseph McBride

VOLUME ONE

J. P. TARCHER, INC.
Los Angeles
Distributed by Houghton Mifflin Company
Boston

Library of Congress Cataloging in Publication Data
Main entry under title:
Filmmakers on filmmaking.

Includes bibliographies.
1. Moving-pictures—Production and direction—Congresses.
2. Moving-picture acting—Congresses.—3. Moving-pictures—Setting
and scenery—Congresses. 4. Costume—Congresses. I. McBride,
Joseph. II. American Film Institute. III. Title: Filmmakers
on filmmaking.
PN1995.9.P7F5 1983   791.43   83-4722
ISBN 0-87477-266-4 (v. 1)
ISBN 0-87477-249-4 (pbk.: v. 1)

Copyright © 1983 by The American Film Institute

Design by Tanya Maiboroda

MANUFACTURED IN THE UNITED STATES OF AMERICA
V 10 9 8 7 6 5 4 3 2 1
First Edition

In memory of James Powers

CREIGHTON
UNIVERSITY

Carl M. Reinert, S.J.
Alumni Memorial Library

Presented By

**Robert E. Kelley, Ph. D.
Class of 1960**

The best of film for me, and the worst of film, is that it is such a collaborative process. You are dealing with incredibly different kinds of people and, even worse than that, you are dependent upon incredibly different kinds of people. I pride myself on having specific conceptions of a film when I decide to do it, and a specific vision of what I want that film to be. But, unlike an author or a composer, I have now become dependent. I am working with a writer, I am working with the actors, I am working with a set designer, I am working with the cameraman, I am working with endless, endless numbers of people. It is enraging at times and it is also the most exciting part of it at times. In the end, if the film is successful, it is a synthesis of so many people that it is impossible to remember who did what and when.

Alan J. Pakula, director

Contents

AMERICAN FILM INSTITUTE SEMINAR WITH BILLY WILDER.

Introduction

This book and its companion volume were drawn from more than a decade of lively discussion between Fellows of The American Film Institute and some of the world's most distinguished filmmakers. Many of the students who participated in the AFI seminars have since become prominent filmmakers themselves—among them, Terrence Malick, Paul Schrader, David Lynch, Amy Heckerling, Jeremy Paul Kagan, Tom Rickman, Matthew Robbins, and Caleb Deschanel—and what they have learned at the AFI has already enriched American film and television. The seminars are an invaluable part of the Fellows' education, an extraordinary opportunity to exchange ideas with masters of the art of filmmaking. To share that experience with the general public, these first two volumes of *Filmmakers on Filmmaking* have been assembled from the more than five hundred seminars held at the AFI since its inception.

The American Film Institute was established in 1967 by the National Endowment for the Arts as an independent, nonprofit national organization to advance the understanding and recognition of the moving image as an art form, to help preserve film and video for future generations, and to develop new talent. With the latter goal in mind, the Center for Advanced Film Studies was opened in Los Angeles in 1969 as a conservatory to teach aspiring filmmakers the basics of their art and craft. The AFI's founding director, George Stevens Jr., said at the dedication of the Center, "While it may not be possible to *train* people to make films, it is possible to create a climate in which people can *learn* to make films." The American professional filmmaking community and prominent visitors from around the world have given generously of their time and expertise to help create that climate of learning for a new generation of filmmakers.

The transcripts of the AFI seminars form a vast repository of oral history, a passing down of knowledge unrivaled in its scope since the beginning of the art form. As director Budd

1

Boetticher told the Fellows in 1970, "What a wonderful advantage it would have been had we had schools like you have here now, where people can ask questions. When I was twenty years old, I didn't get to walk up to John Ford and say, 'Tell me about your last picture.'" And, as cinematographer Howard Schwartz pointed out to the Fellows in 1973, "You don't realize how lucky you are that people want to explain to you how they do things. The whole atmosphere today is different. When I was an assistant cameraman, I had to sneak in on the conversations the director of photography had with his gaffer [chief electrician]. Everybody on the set was secretive. All of this wasn't available then."

Beyond their sheer informative value, the AFI seminars provide many vivid examples of the ways in which a professional filmmaker can share his or her experience for the enlightenment and inspiration of newcomers. Here we have Sidney Poitier telling the moving story of his early struggles to break down the walls preventing members of his race from equal status as filmmakers; Swedish director Ingmar Bergman communicating his joy in sharing the moment of creation with his actors; actress Lucille Ball describing her rise from chorus girl to head of a studio; screenwriter Robert Towne explaining how the clash of creative temperaments on *Chinatown* contributed to the complex mood of that modern film classic; producers Richard Zanuck and David Brown recalling the seemingly endless problems they faced on location for *Jaws*; legendary cinematographer James Wong Howe, after almost sixty years in the industry, retaining his youthful sense of wonderment as he eloquently discusses the nature of light; television producer Norman Lear describing his battles with network censors to bring controversial adult material to the home screen; and many more stories that take the reader inside the creative process of film and television with a rare degree of candor and insight.

If there is a common theme of these many and diverse seminars, it is that filmmaking, for better or worse, is an essentially collaborative process. There may be a dominant personality on or off the set, but even he or she must deal with the necessity of persuading several dozen people to work together for a common goal. While this point may seem an obvious one, it nevertheless has often been overlooked in the literature of film, which has tended to create personality cults around actors and directors at the expense of their less publicized but equally important collaborators such as screenwriters, producers, and cinematographers. *Filmmakers on Filmmaking* attempts to redress that imbalance by giving a comprehensive overview of the various functions involved in making a successful film.

Almost to an individual, the filmmakers who have given seminars at the AFI have been modest and grateful in acknowledging their debt to their fellow craftsmen. The Fellows have heard producer Joseph E. Levine stress that without a good script, no amount of money or effort can produce a good film; Charlton Heston explain the actor's need to depend on the taste and intelligence and skill of his "captain," the director; cinematographer John A. Alonzo give credit to an actor for helping establish the color scheme of a film; editor Verna Fields point out the contributions a musical composer can make to the pacing and emotion of a film; and Ingmar Bergman pay tribute to a producer who gave him the courage and the backing to survive a low point in his career. Throughout these books, filmmakers stress their interdependence with their co-workers and urge the Fellows to banish any thoughts of trying to be a one-man show.

But if filmmakers can also continue to support their claims to be considered artists as well as craftsmen, they must be able to continue finding means of self-expression within the commercial strictures of an impersonal industry; much time in AFI seminars is devoted to discussing that problem. So much, in fact, that Kirk Douglas kidded the Fellows during his 1975 seminar, "I thought I was going to be with a group of artists. All you want to talk about is money. I think you're getting near graduation time." But these concerns are rooted in the hard realities of professional filmmaking, which is, as Charlton Heston puts it, "the only art form in which the artist cannot afford to buy his own tools." The Center for Advanced Film Studies, AFI director Jean Firstenberg has written, teaches aspiring filmmakers the art and craft of their profession "while rooting that learning in the middle ground of the world of commerce. The balance inherent in this undertaking is crucial to the field, reflecting the balance between the work of the artist and the need of the craftsman to find his audience. It is a struggle that mankind has observed in all its art forms, but nowhere so clearly as with the moving image."

During most of the period covered in these volumes, seminars with distinguished guests were held on a weekly basis at the Center for Advanced Film Studies in the AFI's Greystone mansion in Beverly Hills, California; since 1981 the seminars have been held at the new AFI campus, the former Immaculate Heart College in Los Angeles. Each seminar was attended by an average of fifty to seventy-five Fellows, usually in an informal setting with the guest sitting on a couch surrounded by the Fellows. Three of each guest's most important films were screened during the days preceding the seminar so that Fellows would have fresh, specific, and well-informed questions. A few of the seminar transcripts were closed to the public at the request of the guests, but the great majority were inspected and approved by the guests before being made available for public access.

The first two volumes of *Filmmakers on Filmmaking* barely scratch the surface of the wealth of material available. I have been able to include only about 2 percent of the more than 5 million words (forty thousand pages) of transcripts in existence at the AFI's Louis B. Mayer Library on the new campus. This collection alone could provide material for an entire series of books, and the seminars are continuing on a regular basis each month at the Center for Advanced Film Studies.

Several factors governed the choice of seminars for these volumes. It was decided that the best way to reflect the true nature of the filmmaking process would be to include in each volume one representative seminar participant or team from each of several major filmmaking areas: studio executive, producer, director, screenwriter, actor, actress, cinematographer, composer, production designer, costume designer, and editor (although in the last category a second seminar of equal interest did not exist). Other seminars were drawn from such important contributors to films as the agent, the casting director, and the independent filmmaker. Only space limitations prevented the inclusion of seminars with other craftsmen who have shared their expertise with AFI Fellows, including stuntmen, special-effects creators, production managers, makeup artists, and songwriters, as well as seminars with such other figures as bankers, lawyers, laboratory technicians, story editors, publicists, journalists, and critics.

Nearly all of the seminar participants included in these volumes have been involved in an area or areas of filmmaking other than the one for which they are primarily known. It helps to underscore the hybrid nature of filmmaking that, for example, production designer Polly Platt is also a screenwriter; directors Ingmar Bergman, Jean Renoir, and Billy Wilder have also written their own films; Norman Lear, Joseph E. Levine, Richard Zanuck, and David Brown have been at various times both producers and studio executives; editor Verna Fields was also a studio executive; cinematographer John A. Alonzo began as an actor and later directed; Sidney Poitier has had successful careers as both actor and director; and so forth. Production designer Harry Horner, who has also directed, told the Fellows in 1976, "We all should know as much as possible about each other's specialties because, if nothing else, it widens the tolerance of one to the other. . . . The conductor could not work without the orchestra. The members are all on an equal level of importance."

Each of the seminars was considerably longer in transcript than in the edited form that appears here. An average AFI seminar lasts two or three hours and covers sixty or seventy pages of transcript, about three times as long as the average edited seminar in these volumes. To facilitate readability and to provide a clearer line of thought, I have in some instances rearranged material within a seminar (or from more than one seminar by a single participant) and clarified syntax, while still attempting to retain the flavor of conversational rather than written English. Occasional obvious mistakes and confusions of phrasing have been silently corrected, and explanatory background material has been added in brackets, but in no case has the sense of the speaker's words been changed by rewriting. I have, however, taken the liberty of rewriting some of the Fellows' questions to make them simpler, clearer, and more pointed.

As much as possible, I have tried to focus each seminar on topics of general application to the participant's field. Personal anecdotes that help to explain how a filmmaker does his or her particular job have been stressed more than anecdotes of an incidental nature, but care has also been taken to include stories that show how a participant became a filmmaker and how his or her individual artistic personality was formed.

I was faced with some difficult choices in selecting only twenty-four seminars from the more than five hundred available. In some cases it would have been possible to choose equally interesting seminars by other participants, and there the final balance was tipped by the general applicability of a seminar and by its success in relating the participant's craft to the other major filmmaking crafts. To give a taste of the richness of the other material available, some memorable and irresistible moments from other seminars are included in the back of each volume under the heading "Short Subjects."

While this is the first time that AFI seminars have been collected in a book, short versions of seminars have appeared monthly in the AFI's magazine, *American Film*, where portions of several of these seminars previously appeared. Some seminar material also appeared in the previous AFI books *Filmmaking: The Collaborative Art*, edited by Donald Chase, and *Directing the Film: Film Directors on Their Art*, edited by Eric Sherman. The complete seminar transcripts are available for reading by the public at the Louis B. Mayer Library on the campus in Los Angeles; some have also been converted to microfilm, and a few have been made available on videotape.

I wish to express appreciation to all the filmmakers who have given seminars at the AFI; to the AFI Fellows who have participated in them so enthusiastically; and to those people at the AFI most responsible for the ongoing success of the seminar program: AFI director Jean Firstenberg; founding director and current chairman of the Board of Trustees George Stevens Jr.; Center for Advanced Film Studies director Antonio Vellani; former AFI-West director Robert Blumofe; and, especially, the late James Powers, who was head of the seminar program from 1971 until his death in 1980 and conducted many of these seminars. Jim set a tone for the seminars that was both relaxed and serious-minded, and he laid the foundation without which these books could not exist.

Howard Schwartz, who conducts the highly knowledgeable cinematography seminars held by the AFI in conjunction with the American Society of Cinematographers, also deserves thanks, as does the keeper of the seminar transcripts, Anne G. Schlosser, director of the Louis B. Mayer Library. Library assistant Howard Prouty supplied useful information on seminar participants.

The most important assistance in the actual preparation of these books was given by the AFI's director of education services, Peter J. Bukalski, and his staff—Ann Martin, Ronald Mulligan, and Beth Wettergreen. Their patience, diligence, and advice were a constant source of encouragement and support. Jeanine Basinger, professor of film studies at Wesleyan University and a member of the AFI Board of Trustees, gave valuable guidance on the philosophy and content of the books. Eric Sherman and Robert A. Haller advised me on the Stan Brakhage seminar. And, finally, the intelligent and sympathetic editorial contributions of Janice Gallagher and copy editor Georgia Griggs were crucial factors in making these volumes a pleasurable experience.

Los Angeles   *Joseph McBride*
February 1983

THE STUDIO EXECUTIVE
Hal·Wallis

Hal Wallis was responsible for the production of more than two hundred films in his forty-five-year career. During his tenure as a producer and production executive at Warner Brothers, he made such classic films as *Casablanca, Yankee Doodle Dandy, The Maltese Falcon, I Am a Fugitive from a Chain Gang, Little Caesar,* and *The Adventures of Robin Hood.* He later became an independent producer affiliated with Paramount and Universal.

Wallis was a contemporary of such Hollywood giants as Irving Thalberg, Darryl F. Zanuck, and David O. Selznick. Like them, he believed in the supremacy of the producer in all aspects of filmmaking, a philosophy he maintained into the 1970s, despite the demise of the studio system and the general dominance of directors.

Born in 1899, Wallis entered the film business in the early 1920s as a Los Angeles theater manager and soon was hired to run publicity for Warners, then a fledgling studio whose biggest star was Rin Tin Tin. When talkies began, Warners bought the First National Studio in Burbank and Wallis was made production manager. He took the title "in charge of production" in 1933 and kept it until 1942, when his desire for more direct control over his films led him to become an independent producer for the studio. At Warners he oversaw some of the best films of such stars as Bette Davis, James Cagney, Humphrey Bogart, Edward G. Robinson, and Errol Flynn and of such directors as Michael Curtiz, William Wyler, John Huston, Howard Hawks, Raoul Walsh, and Busby Berkeley.

A rift with Jack L. Warner caused Wallis's departure in 1944 for Paramount, where he spent the next twenty-five years. He maintained his strong commercial record with Dean Martin and Jerry Lewis comedies and Elvis Presley musicals, in addition to more prestigious films adapted from the theater, such as *The Rose Tattoo, Becket, Barefoot in the Park,* and *Come Back, Little Sheba.*

In 1969 Wallis began an association with Universal that lasted until 1975, including *Anne of the Thousand Days, Red Sky at Morning, True Grit,* and his most recent film, *Rooster Cogburn.* In 1980 he published his autobiography, *Starmaker.* He is a two-time winner of the Academy of Motion Picture Arts and Sciences' Irving Thalberg Award for distinguished motion-picture producing.

SELECTED FILMOGRAPHY

1930 *The Dawn Patrol | Little Caesar* 1932 *I Am a Fugitive from a Chain Gang* 1933 *Mystery of the Wax Museum | Gold Diggers of 1933 | Footlight Parade | 42nd Street* 1935 *A Midsummer Night's Dream | The Story of Louis Pasteur | Captain Blood* 1936 *Anthony Adverse | Green Pastures | The Charge of the Light Brigade* 1937 *Marked Woman | The Life of Emile Zola* 1938 *Jezebel | The Adventures of Robin Hood* 1939 *Dark Victory | Juarez | The Roaring Twenties* 1940 *The Story of Dr. Ehrlich's Magic Bullet | They Drive by Night | The Sea Hawk | Knute Rockne—All American | The Letter* 1941 *The Sea Wolf | Sergeant York | The Maltese Falcon | They Died with Their Boots On | High Sierra | The Strawberry Blonde | Kings Row* 1942 *Yankee Doodle Dandy | Now, Voyager | Casablanca* 1943 *Air Force | This Is the Army* 1945 *Love Letters | Saratoga Trunk | The Strange Love of Martha Ivers* 1948 *Sorry,*

Wrong Number 1949 *My Friend Irma* 1950 *The Furies* 1952 *Jumping Jacks* 1953 *Come Back, Little Sheba* 1955 *The Rose Tattoo* / *Artists and Models* / *The Rainmaker* 1957 *Gunfight at the O.K. Corral* / *Loving You* 1958 *King Creole* 1960 *G.I. Blues* 1961 *Summer and Smoke* 1962 *Blue Hawaii* 1964 *Becket* 1965 *The Sons of Katie Elder* 1967 *Barefoot in the Park* 1969 *Anne of the Thousand Days* / *True Grit* 1970 *Red Sky at Morning* 1971 *Mary, Queen of Scots* 1975 *Rooster Cogburn*

THE SEMINAR

Hal Wallis held a seminar with the Fellows of the Center for Advanced Film Studies on April 10, 1974.

Perhaps Mr. Wallis would describe a recent project from the beginning through the making of the picture to the end.
WALLIS: Well, I might tie two pictures together, *Becket* and *Anne of the Thousand Days.* I saw Jean Anouilh's play *Becket* in New York and liked it very much. It wasn't picked up quickly by anybody else, so I went back to see it again. I felt there was a great deal of material that was talked about in the second act that could be properly dramatized for a film. I went into negotiations and bought the property, hoping to get Burton and Peter O'Toole to play King Henry II and Becket. I went to Geneva to see Burton. He knew about the property and was interested. He asked who was going to play Henry. I said Peter O'Toole, and he said if that were so, he would do the film, as he admired him greatly. Then I went to London and had a meeting with O'Toole. He asked who was going to play Becket. I said Richard Burton, and he said if that were so, he would do the film, as he admired him greatly. So I made a deal with the two of them on that basis and made the picture.

During the production, I asked Burton if there was any other English history project he would like to do, and he said yes, he had always liked the Maxwell Anderson play *Anne of the Thousand Days.* But he wanted approval of the actress who would play Anne Boleyn. I started negotiations for the play, which were difficult because we had to contact all the heirs of Maxwell Anderson. I finally made the deal, put a writer on it, developed the script, and began looking for an Anne Boleyn. I saw a Canadian film with a brilliant young actress who impressed me very much, Geneviève Bujold. I took the film to England, showed it to Burton, and he approved her, so we went ahead with the project.

Now, from that point on I was involved in everything to do with the production: working on the script with the writer, Edward Anhalt; engaging and working with the art director; doing research; approving and selecting the costumes with Margaret

Furse; casting and scouting for the locations. I went down to Hever Castle in Kent, saw Lord Astor, and got permission to shoot there, which was where Henry VIII actually met Anne Boleyn. Looking for a director, I saw a film I liked that had been made for the Canadian Broadcasting Corporation called *The Young Elizabeth,* directed by Charles Jarrott, who had never done a feature film. I contacted Jarrott in London, had him come up to the hotel, and discussed his directing *Anne.* I liked him and his ideas very much, and the next day I called his agent and hired him.

Now, in shooting that film—as in all of them—I followed through on all phases of production. I am at the studio and on the set every day. I oversee the entire operation. After seeing the dailies, I discuss the previous day's work with the director, approve or suggest improvements, and plan any pickup shots necessary. I am in close contact with the company throughout the day's shooting. If there is any problem, I know it immediately. I work with the production manager, planning the call sheets—the logistics of the next day's shooting, which are extremely complicated on a large-scale period picture such as *Becket* or *Anne.* I work with the editor each day as the picture is shot, and we have close to a first cut within a week or two after the film is finished. I believe in assembling and cutting as you go, because you get a very good feel for the picture: how it is progressing, whether there is anything to be corrected in the performances, the photography, story content, anything. When we go into the final editing, the director of course has the first cut. We usually see the picture together through the various cuts and into the final cut, and then we run it with the composer, spot the music, score, dub, and finally send the print over to Technicolor. When we get back the first answer print [the fully edited film, ready for public screening], we look at that to judge the color balance. So, as you see, I follow the picture through from the time the material is purchased until the print is delivered to the distributing company with whom I am working. *When you first go to make a film, do you have a studio in mind?* **WALLIS:** In my own case, I have, and always have had, a continuing arrangement with the distributing company. First it was Warner Brothers, then it was Paramount, and now it's Universal. Those are the only three companies with which I've been associated. Whenever I find a property and want it, I go out and buy it, knowing the studio will accept it because I have the right to make what I want. I have complete autonomy on my projects.

Your pictures have been exceptionally economical, haven't they, considering that these are costume pictures, with major stars.

WALLIS: I have always believed in doing as much work as possible on paper—in the preparation. Based on my shooting script, I get a budget. I have always, fortunately, come out pretty close to my budget figures. In other words, I don't like to shoot three hours of film, then cut an hour of it, which is very costly, wasteful, and damaging to the overall picture, because there may be gaps in the continuity. I get a good, tight shooting script, time it, budget it, watch the budget, and usually come in pretty much under it.

How much are you personally involved in developing the story structure in that first stage?

WALLIS: I work very closely with the writer. If I buy an original story, I devote a lot of time to conferences with him developing the screen treatment. If I buy a play or a book, I hire a writer and let him prepare a treatment (if I think a treatment is necessary), a step outline, a continuity outline, and a sequence outline. If the material is close enough to screenplay form—like a play—I have him go ahead with a first draft. Then the director and I meet with him on our notes. We begin a series of conferences, rewrites, second and third drafts, and so on, until we come out with our final shooting script. I like a sequence outline, so that you see exactly the direction the story is going to take. In a play, of course, such as *Becket*, the scenes are pretty well laid out. We followed continuity except for that gap between the first and second acts. For example, we dramatized the excommunication, one of the great scenes of the picture, which wasn't seen on the stage.

Do you think it's difficult today for young people interested in producing?

WALLIS: No, I don't. The business is open as never before to new talent and new ideas. Good material is becomingly increasingly hard to find, and if you have a property that appeals to a company or a producer, it would be given every consideration. You could go to Warner Brothers or any studio and say, "I haven't had any experience, but I have this very exciting property. If you're interested, I'll do it with you, or I'll sell it to you, but I want to be a part of it. I want to be an associate on the picture, with a chance to learn and observe." That is done quite frequently.

If a young person wanted to learn the things that go into producing, what would be the best way for him to acquire that knowledge? How did you start as a producer?

WALLIS: I was lucky. I came into the business at the time of its greatest growth. Warner Brothers was expanding and there were many job opportunities. I got a job in the publicity department at the Sunset Boulevard Warner Studios. We made seven pictures a year. There was a closely knit organization, including Jack Warner, Darryl Zanuck, Bill Koenig, and several others. We were all in on everything: the running, cutting, and previewing of pictures. We gradually learned all phases of picturemaking. I think a knowledge of editing is very important for a would-be producer. It teaches you how a film comes together. Knowing something about all the technical aspects of filming is an advantage.

How different is working as a studio producer from working as an independent producer?

WALLIS: Well, as a studio producer, I was in charge of Warner Brothers production for a number of years, and responsible for their entire program, which was considerable. We would be shooting five pictures, editing five, and preparing five or ten at the same time. There was a great deal of work, so we assigned associate producers to individual projects. The load got so heavy, however, that I didn't want to continue carrying it, and I became an independent producer at Warners, producing four pictures a year. During that period I did *Casablanca, Saratoga Trunk, Air Force, Yankee Doodle Dandy, Desperate Journey,* and *Now, Voyager,* among others. I concentrated on one picture at a time, taking a project from the beginning to the end.

When I left there and went to Paramount in my own independent setup, I did the same thing. I had no fixed number of pictures to deliver, no deadlines. When I found a property I wanted to make, I prepared it and shot it. My advice to those of you wanting to become producers is to learn all phases of the business, get experience, observe, and become affiliated with an editor, an associate producer, a screenwriter, or a cinematographer. I think what you're learning here at the American Film Institute is wonderful training for creative producing.

You said before that good material was increasingly hard to find. Why is that, do you think?

WALLIS: Perhaps audiences are more selective now, more sophisticated. Pictures have to be something exceptional today—something different, something important.

Has it changed partly because the studios don't have contract writers and actors?

WALLIS: Possibly. In the early days at Warner Brothers we had a staff of writers, a staff of directors, and a contract list of players. Sound had just been developed, so all the old silent stories and plots seemed new. There was such a market and need for product that writers worked overtime. Directors, producers, and writers worked together in collaboration, inspiring, prodding, stimulating. It was a very productive arrangement. We had under contract actors like James Cagney, Eddie Robinson, Humphrey Bogart, Bette Davis, Olivia de Havilland, George Raft, and Errol Flynn, so that when we made a picture we could cast it from our stock company. Today an unknown actor has a success and immediately acquires a business manager, a lawyer, a tax man, a publicity man —and the man who discovered him can't get him for a picture. The actor works only for his own company. It's not simple anymore.

So it's increasingly difficult to get everything you want to make a good picture.

WALLIS: Difficult, not impossible. In the early days it seemed simpler.

It seems like a lot of producers these days are not creative producers but more like agents—people who put together the package.

WALLIS: Yes, that's true. An agent, a business manager, or someone on the fringes of the business will sell a star or a property or both to a company on the condition that he be the producer of the project involved. But he isn't actually a producer. He's a packager, a promoter.

Do you think that weakens the film?

WALLIS: Well, with that kind of producer they'd better have a strong director, because the producer isn't going to be much help.

Packagers make deals, not pictures. When you find a property, acquire it, work on it from beginning to end, and deliver the finished product as you conceived it, *then* you're producing. A producer, to be worthy of the name, must be a creator.

What do you think a director looks for in a producer?

WALLIS: A collaborator. If a director is sympathetic to working with a producer, he accepts his help in all phases of a project—casting, location hunting, preparation of the script, everything. The concept of the film becomes theirs. They are a two-man team working together toward a single goal. It becomes a collaboration, and a very worthwhile one. I know I have found it so.

Did you at any time want to become a director?

WALLIS: Many times, particularly when I sit in a projection room, watch the rushes, and say to myself, "If I had been on the set, I would have done it another way." But I like what I've done. I like being a producer. I like being involved in all phases of production. And it is creative. As it is, I'm on the set a good deal. But when I work with a director who is talented, who knows his craft, I let him alone far more than I would with a lesser man. I do my job to back him up and give him as much help as I can away from the camera.

What happens if you're on the set and you see a scene going in a direction that you don't think it should go?

WALLIS: I take the director aside and tell him quietly what I think. If there are scenes in the dailies I don't like—if I think they're definitely wrong—I have them done over. If I think there's something off in the performance or we're going wrong in some way, I discuss it with the director. If I feel we need an added shot, a close-up or a two-shot or a movement of the camera, I'll discuss it with him and get what I want. But I don't come down on the set with a whip.

Doesn't the studio, someone higher up, have more to say than a producer on a studio picture?

WALLIS: Luckily, *I've* always been the one higher up. In answer to your question, that used to be true much more so than today. Young filmmakers today have much more freedom of expression once a studio has accepted and approved a project.

When you were at the studio, would you work on a percent of the gross or on a straight salary?

WALLIS: When I was in charge of production, I was on a straight contract deal. When I made my independent deal, which was for Warners, I made a percentage deal.

Would you make more money if you were able to bring in financing from other than the distributor?

WALLIS: Even if it cost more, I would rather go through a distributor and be relieved of negotiations and interest charges involved in outside financing. When the distributor has a stake in the picture, he distributes it to the best advantage. I've worked this way throughout my whole career. I've never tried to make an independent production with outside financing.

You used to make deals with young up-and-coming actors for more than one picture. Do you still try to do that?

WALLIS: It's very difficult to do now because of the changes in the business. I signed Burt Lancaster to his first contract, Kirk Douglas, Shirley MacLaine, Martin and Lewis, Elvis Presley, and we made deals for so many weeks a year, or so many pictures a year, with options for several more years. Today it's almost impossible to do that, because a newcomer who has registered in a film will seldom make a deal for more than one picture, and rarely give options. Actors don't want the restrictions of a contract, even though that was the system that made the great stars.

How much freedom do you allow the director in editing, or supervising the editing, of a film?

WALLIS: As I said before, he has the first cut. He and the editor can put the picture together as he sees it. But it rarely comes to that, because, as I say, I work very closely with the director. The picture is assembled as we go. We have frequent runnings, and we make changes jointly, while the picture is still in production. By the time it's finished, if he wants to make additional changes on his own, he's free to do so.

You've done a very wide scope of things, from Becket *to* Martin and Lewis. *What qualities do you look for in a project?*

WALLIS: I look for projects I feel will make good entertainment. To me that is the prime purpose of a film—to entertain. Many of my films contain messages, but I try to see that the message is delivered entertainingly. When I had a list of stars under contract, I looked for properties tailored to their special talents.

With Elvis Presley, I looked for original stories with colorful backgrounds and situations which lent themselves to musical numbers. I then engaged a team of songwriters who prepared fifteen or twenty songs, of which about five were selected for the picture. For Martin and Lewis, we naturally looked for comedy material suitable for the team. The first one was *My Friend Irma*, which was a radio and television show. I used to say that I made the Martin and Lewis pictures and the Elvis Presley pictures to finance the prestige pictures. But, fortunately, these turned out well, too—pictures like *The Rose Tattoo, Come Back, Little Sheba, Becket,* and others. I have done so many historical dramas lately that I'm looking forward to doing a Western again. My next picture is the sequel to *True Grit,* called *Rooster Cogburn,* starring John Wayne and Katharine Hepburn.

Do you consider the talents of the actors you want to work with and then find a project for them? For example, did you become involved in Mary, Queen of Scots *first, or did you say, "I want to find a property for Vanessa Redgrave"?*

WALLIS: The project came first. In the last scene of *Anne of the Thousand Days,* Anne Boleyn is beheaded because she cannot produce a male heir to the throne. We see her daughter, Elizabeth— later to be queen, ironically—toddling down a garden path and into her place in history. Charles Jarrott and I discussed the possibilities of continuing her story, but, because *The Young Elizabeth* was such a successful television special, decided to pick her up as a grown woman during that episode in history when Mary and Elizabeth were mortal enemies. The scheming and melodrama that went on in that period is more exciting than fiction. I hired a well-known British writer [John Hale] to do an original screenplay, and then signed Glenda Jackson to play Elizabeth and Vanessa Redgrave to play Mary, Queen of Scots.

We've been told there's a golden list of only ten or so actors who are bankable—that is, the stars with whom one can get projects going. Is this true?

WALLIS: If we all waited to cast our films with just the golden ten, there would be only ten films made each year. I think an independent individual producer who has to go to the bank to get money for a picture runs into a problem more often than I do. He is subject to the bank's evaluation of an individual's box-office draw or box-office poison. I don't go by any such list. If I feel an actor is right for a part, I'll use him. Of course, if his record shows he keeps people *out* of the theater, I might be influenced by that. *What genre is most successful at the box office?*

WALLIS: You can't generalize. *True Grit* is one of the most successful I've had. The historical pictures and the Elvis Presley pictures all did the same amount of business, very good business. If there were a formula, it would be very easy. The success of a film depends on how an audience responds to it. It could be the time, casting, subject matter—nobody knows exactly what the ingredients are—but it must be entertaining.

Do you not expect a tremendous box office on a prestige picture like The Rose Tattoo *[from a play by Tennessee Williams] or* Come Back, Little Sheba *[from the William Inge play], or can you hit with artistic successes of this type?*

WALLIS: Both of these pictures were critically and financially successful. In *The Rose Tattoo*, I cast Anna Magnani, who was an unknown quantity here but a big star in Europe, which insured success in the European market. Then I cast Burt Lancaster opposite her; he was a big star here, so we sort of guaranteed our American market with him. In *Sheba*, I cast Shirley Booth, who was a big star on the stage, and put Burt Lancaster opposite her, too, which helped the business. Both Magnani and Booth won Oscars for these films.

There aren't many strong producers anymore. There are strong producer-directors now. Do you feel movies are suffering from this, or do you think this is a good development?

WALLIS: My own opinion is that, with a very few exceptions, most directors would be better off having a strong producer. It takes a great burden off the director. It lets him concentrate on the story, on the actors, on getting the picture on film without being concerned with the endless details that crop up every day in the making of a picture.

Do you feel that two minds are better than one?

WALLIS: Yes, definitely. I feel that being able to discuss things with a producer is helpful to a director. Another opinion is always valuable. When a director cuts a picture, he usually is too involved with the film to be objective. He falls in love with scenes and bits of business that a strong producer might cut for the good of the picture.

Is that why you never got involved with directing?

WALLIS: I might have had to fight with Hal Wallis.

I read in an interview that you objected very strongly to what you called the current trend of violence in the cinema, and yet you produced a lot of gangster movies in the '30s. What do you see as the difference between the gangster movies you produced and the violence you see on the screen today?

WALLIS: Well, gangster pictures in the '30s—*Little Caesar, Roaring Twenties, G-Men,* pictures like that—were stories taken off the front pages. We dramatized them, showed things as they were. They eventually led to reform. Crime never paid in our pictures. In today's pictures, it does. The hero pulls off a caper and gets away with it. Violence and crime are made attractive and desirable.

Do you rely on previews?

WALLIS: To a certain extent. I don't believe in preview cards. When we have previews, we don't pass out cards. We sit in the audience and try to get a gut feel, a reaction from the audience. We listen to their comments when they come out. I find that in passing out cards we're asking for criticism, so we've eliminated that.

Have you ever learned something from a preview that everyone had missed in a screening room?

WALLIS: Yes. A preview can tell you things. You'll sit with an audience and see a cut you should have made, or something in the picture gets a laugh that you didn't think would get a laugh—and shouldn't get a laugh.

What types of things do you want to see a director doing during production?

WALLIS: I like to get a director in on the project as early as possible. For example, *Rooster Cogburn* won't start shooting until September. For me to take on a director at this time [April], five months before production, and then hire him for ten or twelve weeks of shooting, becomes almost financially impossible. So what I try to do is give the director the script, get his general ideas, have meetings with him, let the work progress, have him look at the locations, and then have him come in sufficient time before production to concentrate on casting and his own work.

When he comes in just before production, what have you already accomplished?

WALLIS: By then the script is usually in pretty good shape. We have lists of actors, possibilities for all parts, which we talk about. We'll have interviews and quite a bit of preparation to do. I have my production manager out now looking for locations. He was in Arkansas last week and is in Georgia today. He's coming back here and then he's going up to Oregon and Washington. He's photographing locations that should fit the action throughout the script. I will go over all of those with him, and then I will probably go see the ones that are the best possibilities.

With the director or by yourself?

WALLIS: I'll go with the director. I prefer to.

Have you already decided how much the picture should cost?

WALLIS: Yes, $4.5 million. When I plan a picture, I know from experience approximately what it will cost. I break the script down into scenes and have it budgeted. If the cost is too high, I make cuts, change locations, whittle down until the price is right and reasonable for a profitable return. I try to evaluate the potential and combine a business approach with the artistic. When you know how much the picture should do, you spend accordingly. If you know you're going to lose money on it, there's no point in making it.

When you're deciding whether to shoot on location or in a studio, what are the advantages and disadvantages? Which do you prefer?

WALLIS: For *Rooster* we need rapids and mountains, and we'll probably be shooting in Oregon or Washington. As a general rule, it's far better to use actual locations because they give a sense of reality to a picture. In some cases, it isn't possible. Certain sequences have to be shot on a stage or on a studio back lot. If you're blowing up a building or a car, you do it on the back lot, where the explosions and fire can be controlled.

Isn't it cheaper to film outside the studio?

WALLIS: No, locations are quite expensive. You travel with an army—any number of trucks, station wagons, cars, eighty to a hundred people on a crew. You have to transport them, you have to house them, and it's a *very* expensive operation.

In the more than forty years you've been in the business, and over two hundred films you've made, are there any films you have a special fondness for?

WALLIS: *Casablanca* is probably my favorite. *Yankee Doodle Dandy, Kings Row, The Maltese Falcon, True Grit, G.I. Blues, Barefoot in the Park,* and *Red Sky at Morning* were all fun to make, and memorable. Actually, the next one is always my favorite one.

I read that Casablanca *was written as it was being shot, and you didn't know the ending. How did that come about?*

WALLIS: We never dreamed *Casablanca* would become a classic. We started out to make a good picture. I wanted Ingrid Bergman to play opposite Bogart. I had to borrow her from David O. Selznick [the producer who had her under contract], and it was very difficult at that time to borrow anybody from him. I chased him from Malibu to New York and back, and made a two-picture deal for her—*Casablanca* and *Saratoga Trunk.* She and Bogie were so great together.

We did have problems on *Casablanca*—writing problems. And we did make changes in that script all the way through the production. It was a stage play, but I don't think it was ever produced. It was called *Everybody Comes to Rick's*—ever heard of it? An inconsequential play about a saloonkeeper in Casablanca. All the intrigue in the area took place at Rick's. We started with just that. The writers [Julius and Philip Epstein, Howard Koch, and Casey Robinson] used to meet in my office after the day's shooting, and we kicked the script around until it finally worked. There was a long discussion about how to end it, whether Bergman should go away with Paul Henried or whether she should stay with Bogart. We could see ending it either way, but finally decided to have her do the decent thing and go with her freedom-fighter husband.

Did you shoot it both ways?

WALLIS: No, we didn't shoot it, we discussed it.

Were other directors considered besides Michael Curtiz?

WALLIS: No. And, incidentally, he was one of the great ones. He was a master with a camera, way ahead of his time. He could do anything. He would do a picture like *Casablanca, The Charge of the Light Brigade, The Sea Hawk,* musicals, comedies—a fantastic man. He did one picture after another for me. He was never happy unless he was working. On the last day of shooting a film, he'd ask when he could start the next one. He was tireless.

Do you prefer finding a novel or a play or a screenplay?

WALLIS: It's a lot simpler to make a picture from a finished piece of material such as a book or a play because you start with more than just an idea. If it's a play, you've seen it produced on the stage. A book has description, dialogue, situations, everything worked out in black and white. When you start with an original piece of material, all that has to be created. For example, *Gunfight at the O.K. Corral,* though based on history, was inspired by an article in *Holiday* magazine—nonfiction. It was about the strange relationship between the leading lawman, Wyatt Earp, and the leading gunslinger, Doc Holliday, the admiration they had for one another. I bought the article and hired Leon Uris to do the screenplay as an original. We went into research, found what had happened with Wyatt and his rivals, the Clantons, and embellished what I had bought. But it was a thin piece of material to start with, just a magazine article. I like working that way sometimes.

Do you or the distribution company use market-analysis services to test a property for public opinion before starting the production?

WALLIS: I go by gut instinct. Either I like it or I don't. If I like it, see a picture in it that can be entertaining, then I buy it. I've never cared for that analysis routine.

How many scripts come through your company? Are your readers reading a great deal of material?

WALLIS: Yes, and I do a lot of reading. I get synopses on all material that is published, forecasts from publishers of what they expect to bring out soon with brief outlines of what the stories are about. If I'm interested, I send for the complete material. Occasionally I get galleys directly from the publisher, and the competition for material is very keen, because everybody is looking for properties. If you do find something, you have to act very quickly.

I had a strange situation on *True Grit.* When the book came out, the agent sent seven copies of galleys to seven different people in Hollywood. I got one. The response was so great that he sent out a wire stating he would send a telegram on a certain day, giving the price, and if more than one company met the price, the author reserved the right to choose whom he wanted to have it. I wired and said I would accept it, as did about five other companies. The author, Charles Portis, was traveling in a jeep somewhere down in Central America. He goes off frequently to Mexico and Central America, and his agent didn't hear from him for a week. When he finally reached him, Portis said he wanted me to have the property. Very fortunate.

Did you ever find out why they wanted your company as opposed to the others?

WALLIS: They had probably seen *Gunfight* and *Last Train from Gun Hill* and some of the other Western pictures I'd made. Duke Wayne's company was one that put in a bid. When I heard he wanted it, all I did was pick up the telephone and say, "I've got it, do you want to do it?" He did.

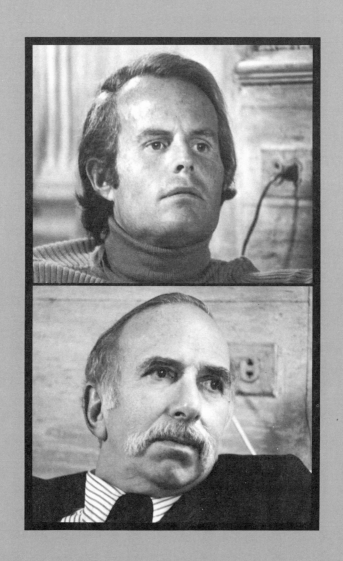

Richard Zanuck and David Brown

Among the most powerful producers in contemporary filmmaking, Richard Zanuck and David Brown combine backgrounds in Hollywood studio production and the New York literary world. They first worked together as 20th Century-Fox executives in the 1950s, during the reign of Zanuck's late father, Darryl F. Zanuck.

Richard Zanuck, born in 1934, served his apprenticeship in the story and publicity departments of Fox before acquiring his first production experience as an assistant to the producer on *Island in the Sun* and *The Sun Also Rises* in 1957. He became a full-fledged producer on *Compulsion* in 1959 and followed with *Sanctuary* and *The Chapman Report* before assisting his father on the 1962 World War II epic, *The Longest Day*. The younger Zanuck was elevated to vice-president in charge of production in 1967 and, after an internecine battle with his father for control of the studio, ascended to the presidency in 1969.

David Brown, born in 1916, spent twenty-five years in the journalism field, as a reporter on the San Francisco *News* and *The*

Wall Street Journal and then as editor-in-chief of *Liberty* magazine and managing editor of *Cosmopolitan* (which is now edited by his wife, Helen Gurley Brown). He entered the film business in 1952 as managing editor of the Fox story department and spent the next ten years in various executive capacities in the department and on the staff of the elder Zanuck. After departing for a brief stint in book publishing, he returned to Fox in the mid-1960s and was executive vice-president for creative operations while Richard Zanuck was head of the studio. Among the films Fox made during that period were *The Sound of Music, Butch Cassidy and the Sundance Kid, Patton*, and *M*A*S*H*.

They left for executive positions at Warner Brothers in 1971, but resigned the following year to form their own production company. After making a horror film and a black exploitation film, they hit paydirt in 1973 with *The Sting* and followed it two years later with *Jaws*, which became the largest-grossing film in motion-picture history until it was surpassed by *Star Wars*. The Zanuck/Brown Company became affiliated with 20th Century-Fox in 1980.

JOINT FILMOGRAPHY
(as producers)

1973 *Sssssss* / *Willie Dynamite* / *The Sting*   1974 *The Sugarland Express* / *The Black Windmill* / *The Girl from Petrovka* 1975 *The Eiger Sanction* / *Jaws*   1977 *MacArthur*   1978 *Jaws 2* 1980 *The Island*   1982 *The Verdict*

THE SEMINAR

Richard Zanuck and David Brown held a seminar with the Fellows of the Center for Advanced Film Studies on April 17, 1975.

How do you divide your work?
ZANUCK: We don't divide it. David is based in New York, I'm located out here, and whenever there is a production, one of us is always there. So we don't divide it in any definitive way at all.
BROWN: That way neither of us can get the blame.
ZANUCK: We've been on the road with the paperback edition of *Jaws*, and we've been on these TV shows and the talk shows where people call in and ask questions, and one question that was asked wherever we went was "What is a producer?" It seems that the role of the producer today, and very often in the past, has been overlooked and forgotten. When you think of the people who really founded the business, the great founders of the studios, they were producers—and very creative people. But today, even within the industry, people don't know what a producer does.
BROWN: Perhaps the most important qualification of a producer —far more important than his knowledge of the technology of motion pictures—is his ability to detect a story that has both artistic and commercial appeal, and his ability to evaluate and attract the right directors and writers. The producer is, first of all, the man with the dream. Sometimes he is part promoter, but if he is a true producer he not only finds the property but also works on all versions of the script. Mr. Zanuck and I find no area of the film too mundane for us to become involved in. After years of being generals and having run production companies, we learned to be generalists. Now we've had an opportunity to get into the guts of the film, and we very much oppose the notion that all producers are money men, that producers are basically promoters.
Do you have different points of view on what you think would make a good picture?
BROWN: Frequently. And each of us has a veto. Mostly we talk it out. We go through a period of discarding a project and coming back to it and discarding it, that kind of decision making. What we refer to as "the big yes" comes infrequently. It came on *Jaws* and it came on *The Sting*, and, in our executive careers, on *Butch*

Cassidy and the Sundance Kid, which we read and acquired over-night. *M*A*S*H* was an unqualified big yes. *Patton* was not a big yes. *Patton* was a very slow yes.

ZANUCK: It took twenty years to happen.

BROWN: It was a long yes with many nos in between.

But is there any one particular element that you immediately go for?

BROWN: Entertainment. But we are very poor at doing genre films for the sole purpose of making money. We discovered that we make them too good and too expensive, so we try to select subjects of some distinction. We want to contribute to film literature. This is something that's not often realized about producers who have a good commercial track record.

Mr. Brown, how has your career in journalism helped you?

BROWN: It's made me alert to sources of material. It's created relationships with authors, editors, and publishers. And it's made me sensitive to opinion, world opinion, and social pressures. Since I was always a popular journalist, it's made me sort of a mass-appeal authority.

I can't emphasize too strongly that a producer is a fellow with an idea. He doesn't have to have a bankroll. If you are a man or a woman with an idea, there's every opportunity for you to produce films, but you must work out the idea. If you do a treatment, make it an eighty-page treatment. Don't give somebody a paragraph or say "I've got a great idea for a film." The difference is the follow-through. Without that the more talented person frequently fails to score.

If you were just beginning now and didn't have a track record, what would you do differently in terms of initiating a project?

ZANUCK: You've got to hustle with the literary people. You've got to get the material. Because without material you're just you.

BROWN: I'll give you an example of how it can be done. Sometimes you have to get some financial backing. Tony Bill [an actor-turned-producer] heard David Ward [a screenwriter] talk about his "con" project. He got David Ward to put a great deal of it on cassettes, and then, as I understand it, he got together with Julia and Michael Phillips [with whom Bill previously produced *Steel-yard Blues*] and they financed the writing of the script that became *The Sting.* The material that made the world's third-largest grossing film [at that time] did not come as the result of a high-priced auction at a New York literary agency or in Hollywood. Tony Bill simply saw something in it and steered it to the right people. People have walked into drugstores and picked up paper-backs which became John Wayne Westerns. Money is good only when you have judgment—otherwise every studio in town would be making a fortune. The main thing to do is to get to know writers, people who can write a screenplay.

As for finding hit material, I think you have to have a flair for what's popular. The primitive showmen of Hollywood, who frequently came from other businesses and some of whom could barely speak English, knew precisely what interested people, what involved an audience. You know it or you don't. When people come to us and say, "This'll make a good picture," we say, "That's not enough." Nobody's looking for just a good picture now, be-cause television commands so much attention. Even if you can get a studio to back a nice little film—or a nice big film—that can be done just as effectively on television, no one will go and see it in a theater. Television is the great adversary these days.

Film is called the "director's medium." How do you relate to the director in getting the story together and after the film starts shooting?

ZANUCK: Most of our influence with directors is in the early stages of writing the screenplay. The director is in charge of the set. We don't hover over his shoulder.

Do you push him in a certain direction, though?

BROWN: We select a director for what we believe a director can do for a film. And we operate—we hope—as effective buffers. *We* take the punishment if we're over budget, if we're over schedule. We keep our director and our cast in protective custody.

There's no day that one of us—or more frequently both of us—is not on the set or on the location. We conduct our other busi-ness wherever we're shooting, but we are totally aware of what's going on. We make suggestions and try to solve problems without interfering with the director's work.

But suppose the director's going over budget? How do you deal with that?

BROWN: Once a budget and schedule have been approved and then there are overpowering reasons for going over budget or over schedule, we exercise our authority cautiously. We try to keep up the morale of the company. We try to evaluate what is waste and what is not waste. The director is more involved than anyone else in the financial side of the film; shooting time is the prime costly ingredient. But we have no hesitation, either Mr. Zanuck or I, in telling the director that he's doing a sequence which will never be used. We try logic and persuasion. And if he insists, I suppose we would have to say, "We can't let you do it." But he will come to you with his problems, and he will value your opinion and support, if you can draw a fine line between your responsibility to your backers and your responsibility to your director and the film.

Do you allow your director to have total authority over editing?

ZANUCK: In most cases the studio has the final cut. We don't have it as producers, nor does the director have it. In very rare cases, the director has the final cut within certain parameters: he has to bring in the film within a certain length, and it's got to get a certain rating. We work closely with him after he has presented his first cut. If there are discrepancies and differences of opinion, they are flushed out in previews.

What influences you in your choice of a director for a particular film?

BROWN: In the case of *Jaws*, we knew that it could be effectively directed, and maybe more economically directed, by an "engineer"-type director. But we were looking for a film as well as a movie, and that's why we selected Steven Spielberg. At first Spielberg was reluctant to take on *Jaws* because he recognized it would be primarily a commercial movie and not necessarily a distinguished film, and he is a serious filmmaker. Dick and I convinced him, and I think he now realizes he did make a film as well as a movie—not that he doesn't respect the big commercial movie and regard it as a necessary part of his career.

ZANUCK: We'd met Spielberg at Fox briefly. I was very impressed by him after seeing his short, *Amblin'*. This was pre-*Duel* [Spielberg's acclaimed 1971 TV movie]. He'd brought a project over there, *The Sugarland Express*, which he had co-authored with Hal Barwood and Matt Robbins and very much wanted to direct. He didn't direct it at Fox, and we left. During the process of acquiring the property at Universal, we talked extensively. It was a combination of our belief in the property and the story and our belief in Steve that swung us [*Sugarland Express* was Spielberg's first theatrical feature].

As independent producers working with the studio's money, going over budget or over schedule affects you in the financial sense. In terms of working with Universal and taking the extra time to do Jaws *right, were you concerned with clauses in your contract that might penalize you financially?*

ZANUCK: One is always concerned when going over budget. We are concerned in regard to our credibility as producers when a picture is going over budget like that picture went over budget. We don't have any penalty clause in our contract. We can always be removed, literally removed. They can always send a wire saying "We're not going to ship any more film" or "We're going to take the cameras away" or "Make the rest of the picture on the back lot."

BROWN: Many creative decisions are made by the studio. During *M*A*S*H*, Dick was head of the studio and I was the second man, but we functioned as executive producers on all films. Our decision not to go to Korea with *M*A*S*H*, and to shoot it on the Fox Ranch in Malibu, turned out, I think, to be a sound artistic decision. A film like that, somewhat larger than life, needed the stylized feeling of an unrealistic setting.

ZANUCK: I remember arguing with the director, Robert Altman, about that. He had finally agreed but was holding out to go to Japan for the one golf course scene. I decided to go across the street from Fox to a public golf course and dress up a few people to look like Japanese women caddies. It worked fine.

BROWN: I'd like to underscore that the producer makes a distinct contribution to filmmaking. Before the filming of *Jaws*, Steven Spielberg and the two of us had a very thorough discussion about the style of photography. We did not want what was done brilliantly and appropriately by Vilmos Zsigmond in *The Sugarland Express*. This was a different kind of story. We had the sea. We had the special effects. This film required a straightforward photographic style—fortunately and happily, Steve's idea all along. The tone, the taste, the director's choices for cameraman, art director—all the key decisions—must be seconded by the producers. And if we differ, we're not afraid to make our differences known.

You received "presentation" credit on The Sting. *How did you become involved with the producers and why did they come to you?*

ZANUCK: *The Sting* came about through a relationship that David and I had with Tony Bill and Michael and Julia Phillips at Warner Brothers when we were there as executives. Shortly after we left Warners, they came to us and said they had what they thought was a very good screenplay, but they were a little shaky after *Steelyard Blues*. It hadn't turned out as they had hoped. They wanted some guidance on how to set this up. David and I then made our deal at Universal, and presented that as one of the projects. Then, in association with Bill and the Phillipses, we put together the cast and director George Roy Hill.

Could you take a film you've done and talk it all the way through?

ZANUCK: Sure. Let's take *Jaws* because it's current. David and I both received the manuscript at the same time as a few other people in the business. It was right off Peter Benchley's typewriter. David was in New York, I was in Los Angeles. We read it immediately, as we'd had some advance word that it was something special and hot. We decided independently that it was highly commercial, unique, and something that would interest us as producers. Within twenty-four hours we were well into negotiations. We found ourselves in the middle of a fierce bidding contest with some other very important people. We did everything. We got down on bended knee. We made a lot of promises that, happily, we lived up to.

What kind of promises?

ZANUCK: We tried to sell Benchley on using us through his agent, because we didn't know Peter at that time. The other people had as much money as we did. It got down to who was going to make the better picture. We convinced him that we would. We worked with Peter on a first-draft screenplay, and after that was completed we selected Steven as the director. He worked with us and Benchley on a second-draft screenplay. We changed some of the personal story from the book because we found that what worked as a book didn't necessarily work as a film. But we created other problems for ourselves in the second and third acts. [Carl Gottlieb did additional work on the screenplay on location throughout the shooting.]

We then started to tackle the really enormous physical problems of having to put this on the screen. It was like building Apollo One. We're talking about a twenty-five-foot shark, no animation, no miniatures, but a twenty-five-foot shark that has to do all kinds of wild things. And the secret of the movie was that the shark had to be real. Otherwise, the movie wouldn't have worked. The shark had to do everything, including jump out of the water and into the boat.

BROWN: While munching away.

ZANUCK: And the terrifying question was always out there in front of us—simply, Would this thing work? We were fighting a start date. We had to get to Martha's Vineyard [Massachusetts], which we had selected as the best place to shoot the film, by a certain date so that we could get in and out before the tourists came. As it turned out, we were there before the tourists, during the tourist season, and we said goodbye to the tourists. A lot of them spent a very fine summer playing extras in the picture. We lived through five months on the island, and everything eventually did work.

BROWN: When we bought the rights to the book and reread it, we said to each other: How do we do it? How do you get that shark to do those things? How do you get a man to be swallowed by a shark? And when we asked the production wizards, they said, "We don't know."

ZANUCK: Then we asked the special-effects wizards, and they didn't know either. But we found Robert Mattey, a retired wizard from Disney, and he did it for us. It took thirteen men to operate the shark behind a big console. We fought weather, we fought the sea, we fought the tide. Due to Steve's brilliance and the expertise of Robert Mattey, you can't tell our shark from the real shark. It makes the picture work beautifully.

BROWN: And, for some peculiar reason, the actual great white shark is not as real looking to the lay eye as our shark. We've had to downgrade our own so that they would match the actual great white, on which we have a great deal of footage in the film. The making of this film was one of the most complex syntheses of specialized skills in film history. We had to trust people who were dealing in technical matters we couldn't understand: saline content, reverse polarity of electrical systems. All we said was, "Let's keep going."

ZANUCK: "Until they stop us." But to conclude your question, we're still working on the film to this day, and we will until it's in the theaters. That's our job.

What do you do when you get halfway through something like Jaws and all of a sudden the weather is terrible, you're having difficulties, and your budget's tripled?

BROWN: Pray and press on. You lie a little. We even considered suspending production to gather our strength and return in the fall. However, experience told us to press on. And at no time was there an airlift of executives from the MCA/Universal Black Tower [the film industry nickname for the conglomerate's headquarters on the Universal lot]. At no time was there an ultimatum: "What are you doing with that fish?" At no time did they say, "Shoot it in Griffith Park lake"—if there *is* a lake in Griffith Park [a traditional Los Angeles location of which it is said "A tree is a tree, a rock is a rock; shoot it in Griffith Park"].

ZANUCK: There is a lake on the back lot.

BROWN: *Jaws* is an example of studio trust, and it is an example of what producers can do with their much-battered credibility. There were times, I'm sure, when they thought we were insane, and there were times when we thought we were, too. But we were determined to get everything on screen that was in the book.

You don't go over the script and say, "We've got to cut this scene and we can't have the star here—it's going to cost extra"?

ZANUCK: No. We cut, as we do all scripts, and we time pictures as we're making them. If we were running over length, we would then examine what had not been shot to see what was absolutely necessary. That went on with *Jaws*. But we wouldn't just cut sequences for financial reasons.

BROWN: We actually embellished. Mr. Spielberg found new things for our sharks to do that they were never designed to do. With the wizardry we had at hand, we redesigned as the challenge grew. We always try to preserve a kind of flexibility for the director. We don't say, "Well, why didn't you tell us back in Universal City that you wanted a double left turn?"

ZANUCK: As the challenge grew, the budget grew.

I was living in Boston at the time the photography on Martha's Vineyard was taking place. I remember an interview with Spielberg in a Boston newspaper; he said, "We have all these problems and we don't know how it's going to end yet. But we'll figure it out." Wouldn't that make the most terrific tension for you as the producers?

ZANUCK: I don't know that particular story, but I think if the studio had honestly believed we didn't have an ending to the picture, the Lear jets would've landed at Martha's Vineyard.

BROWN: There are two ways, apparently, to make a movie. One is to have a script, as Alfred Hitchcock always has, in which every frame of the movie is indicated. The other way is the collaborative process where you have a good script but you try to make it better and you try to adjust it to the realities and opportunities of the location. The script can either be a work in progress or frozen at the beginning of principal photography. I'm not saying one is better than the other; I'm just saying there are those two ways of doing movies. Mr. Hitchcock told us that he would no more improvise during shooting than the conductor of the New York Philharmonic would improvise while conducting. He believes the time to improvise is when you're working with paper, not film. Those are the choices.

Jaws is going to have a massive advertising campaign, with a tremendous amount of money spent on a very short but intense nationwide opening. Who made that decision, and what participation did you have in it?

ZANUCK: Universal consulted us on those decisions, but they have final say. *Jaws* is going to be released in about five hundred theaters with a very intensive initial television exposure campaign, probably the biggest of all time. Plus, the deals they've made with the picture are extraordinary. The shortest deal in any theater is nine weeks, so it'll play the entire summer.

Was this campaign your initiative, or did they bring it to you?

BROWN: It was devised by Universal. It's a revolutionary theory, actually. The old idea was to take a class film, which we hope this is, as well as a mass film, and open it first in New York, probably at an East Side house, then in Westwood [the location of UCLA], and then let the media percolate the word that it's a great hit. *The Godfather* broke that pattern because of the public's urgency to see it. Paramount released *The Godfather* simultaneously in many houses that had previously never played anything but single exclusive engagements. It has become apparent to the distributors that they can get their money back faster, and satisfy the urgency to see a film, by adopting a broader release pattern. When you have a film like *Jaws*, where there is apparently a great deal of interest, why wait? Why make them wait six months or a year? Why make them stand in line with no hope of getting in and then go away, perhaps never to return? Make it available to the public. In the case of *The Sting*, even though we had Paul Newman and Robert Redford and George Roy Hill, it still opened more slowly. We had to get word-of-mouth out to the public. We didn't want to take the chance of having it overexposed until it started to build—which it did.

Do you believe in changing a film after a preview?

ZANUCK: We have gone to over two hundred previews altogether. I used to think that previews were vital, but now I think previews are vital for certain kinds of pictures and not for others. I think it's dangerous to release a drama without a preview; there might be a bad laugh of some kind. *Jaws*, which we did preview in Dallas and Long Beach, California, really didn't need to be previewed. I used to believe in cards, but I don't anymore. I can tell a great deal by seeing if people are fidgety and moving around, getting up to get a Coke or something. I don't think cards are sophisticated enough, and I think we're asking too much. The average viewer suddenly becomes Judith Crist. To be too influenced by cards can be dangerous.

BROWN: I find previews very important in giving friendly persuasion to your distributor—and to the producers—to back the film all the way. There are things that can be done to the film if the preview audience tells you you're in trouble. Generally, you can't change the course of history too much, but you can improve the film. But if you have a fortunate preview, as we had with *Jaws* and *The Sting*, all the wheels will start turning just a little faster.

ZANUCK: Out of all the films I've previewed, I'd say that one rule comes through very strongly: when you have a lousy preview, I mean a really lousy preview, that picture is not going to make it. Very rarely. The only exception I can remember—and it wasn't a good picture—was *Valley of the Dolls*. It had a terrible preview and yet turned out to be a big hit. But the reverse can happen. You have a sensational preview, all the cards are great and the audience is cheering, everybody is opening champagne, and the picture goes out and dies. It happened with *Star!*

BROWN: If the preview ad hints at the identity of the film, such as "a major-studio preview based on the number-one best-selling novel by Peter Benchley about a great white shark—"

ZANUCK: A subtle ad.

BROWN: If the identity of the film is sufficiently known—unlike previews that are truly sneaks—such a preview will tell you whether the people will come or not. In Dallas, where we previewed *Jaws*, there were perhaps two thousand people standing in a hailstorm, waiting in line three hours before show time with the prospect of seeing *The Towering Inferno* first, to ensure that they would get to see *Jaws*. We had to schedule a second preview at eleven P.M. to keep the crowds content.

What can be done to help small films by first-time directors that start slowly at the box office, such as Pretty Poison *[1968, directed by Noel Black and made at Fox when Zanuck and Brown were executives there] or* The Sugarland Express?

ZANUCK: *Pretty Poison* is a favorite of mine, and it was a favorite of the critics. The distribution department had claimed it a total failure. We even rereleased the picture after everybody had read the reviews. Unfortunately, the results were not much better.

BROWN: There's no way, apparently, to outguess the public. There is a certain justifiable cynicism among distributors and studios. That's another function of the producer—to get the studio to do all the things the director claims are never done for the obscure film or the first film or the film that's failing. But in the case of *Pretty Poison* everything was done.

In the case of *Sugarland Express*, Universal gave Spielberg and us carte blanche in developing advertising and getting outside creative shops, to avoid that studio look. Our early ads were our own; Spielberg himself shot one of them. Our campaigns didn't work. We learned that any ad with a gun is anathema to the East Side public on Third Avenue in New York City. On Broadway, however, show lots of guns. We learned a great deal. But the point is that to this very day, far from giving up on the film, Universal has continued to try to find ways of making it work. So a young new director is not necessarily shortchanged.

Why do you think The Girl from Petrovka *was a failure at the box office?*

BROWN: We had originally designed *The Girl from Petrovka* as a film to be made in the Soviet Union. That was the excitement of it. We were finally kicked from one country to another right back to the back lot. But that isn't the reason the picture didn't work. We made a mistake. The subject was a Cold War concept that was passé.

ZANUCK: It's easy to look back and see where you went wrong. And it's also just as mystifying to us to see a picture like *The Sting*, which we're tremendously proud of, do that historic business. We'd be the first ones to admit that, frankly, it's extraordinary. There are great mysteries in this business.

BROWN: Thank heavens.

THE DIRECTOR
Ingmar Bergman

Ingmar Bergman is universally regarded as one of the masters of contemporary filmmaking. The films he has written and directed have attained a rare degree of moral and psychological insight, and the performances he has evoked from his actors and actresses are among the most vivid and intense in film history.

The Swedish filmmaker first came to international prominence in 1956 with his medieval morality play, *The Seventh Seal.* By that time he had already directed seventeen films, including such diverse major works as *Summer with Monika, The Naked Night,* and *Smiles of a Summer Night.*

Born in 1918, the son of a Protestant minister, Bergman made his debut as a professional stage director in 1944, the same year his first screenplay, *Torment,* was directed by Alf Sjöberg. Bergman directed his first film, *Crisis,* the following year.

As a filmmaker, Bergman has managed to sustain a high degree of creative freedom. He almost always bases his films on his own original screenplays, and he often works with his "stock company" of actors, including Max von Sydow, Bibi Andersson, Ingrid Thulin, Harriet Andersson, Gunnar Björnstrand, and Liv

Ullmann. He has maintained equally loyal and fertile collaborations with cameramen Gunnar Fischer and Sven Nykvist.

Since *The Seventh Seal,* Bergman's most acclaimed films have included his religious trilogy—*Through a Glass Darkly, Winter Light,* and *The Silence*—as well as *Wild Strawberries, The Virgin Spring, Persona, The Shame, A Passion, Cries and Whispers, Scenes from a Marriage, The Magic Flute,* and *Autumn Sonata.* He has also directed many notable stage plays in Sweden, London, Paris, and Munich, and he was head of the Royal Dramatic Theater in Stockholm from 1963 to 1966.

In 1975 Bergman left Sweden because of tax problems. Although they were later resolved, he established a permanent residence in Munich and did not make another film in his native land until *Fanny and Alexander* (1982). His AFI seminar was conducted on his first visit to Hollywood, shortly after he left Sweden.

SELECTED FILMOGRAPHY

1945 *Crisis*   1949 *Prison / Thirst / To Joy*   1950 *Summer Interlude*   1952 *Summer with Monika*   1953 *The Naked Night* 1954 *A Lesson in Love*   1955 *Smiles of a Summer Night*   1956 *The Seventh Seal*   1957 *Wild Strawberries*   1958 *The Magician* 1959 *The Virgin Spring*   1961 *Through a Glass Darkly*   1962 *Winter Light*   1963 *The Silence*   1966 *Persona*   1968 *Hour of the Wolf / The Shame*   1969 *A Passion*   1971 *The Touch* 1973 *Cries and Whispers / Scenes from a Marriage*   1975 *The Magic Flute*   1976 *Face to Face*   1977 *The Serpent's Egg*   1978 *Autumn Sonata*   1980 *From the Life of the Marionettes*   1982 *Fanny and Alexander*

THE SEMINAR

Ingmar Bergman held a seminar with the Fellows of the Center for Advanced Film Studies on October 31, 1975.

Please tell us how you work with actors.
BERGMAN: It can be a very complicated question, and it can be a very simple question. If you want to know exactly how I work together with my actors I can tell you in one minute: I just use my intuition. My only instrument in my profession is my intuition. When I work at the theater or in the studio with my actors I just *feel*; I don't *know* how to handle the situation, how to collaborate with the artists, with the actors. One thing is very important to me: that an actor is always a creative human being, and what your intuition has to find out is how to make free—do you understand what I mean?—to make free the power, the creative power in the actor or the actress.

I can't explain how it works. It has nothing to do with magic; it has a lot to do with experience. But I think when I work together with the actors I try to be like a radar—I try to be wide open—because we have to create something together. I give them some stimulations and suggestions and they give me a lot of stimulations and suggestions, and if this fantastic wave of giving and taking is cut off for any reason I have to feel it and I have to look for the reason—good heavens, what has happened?—and I know if we try to work with those waves cut off it is terrifying; it is the hardest, toughest job that exists, both for me and the actors. Some directors work under aggression: the director is aggressive and the actors are aggressive, and they get marvelous results. But to me it is impossible. I have to be in contact, in touch with my actors the whole time. Because what we first of all create when we start a work together is an atmosphere of security around us. And it's not only me who creates that atmosphere; we are together to create it.

But you know, all those situations, all those decisions, all those very difficult decisions, you have to make hundreds of them every day—I never think. It's never an intellectual process, it's just intuition. Afterward you can think it over—What was this? What was that? You can think over every step you have made.
Do you write in the same way?

BERGMAN: Yes, yes, yes. The best time in the writing, I think, is the time when I have no ideas about how to do it. I can lie down on the sofa and I can look into the fire and I can go to the seaside and I can just sit down and do nothing. I just play the game, you know, and it's wonderful and I make some notes and I can go on for a year. Then, when I have made the plan, the difficult job starts: I have to sit down on my ass every morning at ten o'clock and write the screenplay. And then something very, very strange happens: often the personalities in my scripts don't want the same thing I want. If I try to force them to do what I want them to do, it will always be an artistic catastrophe. But if I let them free to do what they want and what they tell me, it's OK.

So I think that is the only way to handle it, because all intellectual decisions must come afterward. You have seen *Cries and Whispers*, yes? For half a year, I went around and I just had a picture inside about three women walking around in a red room in white clothes and I didn't know why. I couldn't understand these damned women—I tried to throw it away, I tried to write it down, I tried to find out what they said to each other, because they whispered. And suddenly it came out that they were watching another woman who was dying in the next room, and then it started. But it took about a year. It always starts with a picture with some kind of tension in it, and then slowly it comes up.

In your films you often confuse reality and dreams, and I wonder if you feel that they are of equal importance.

BERGMAN: You know, you can't find in any other art, and you can't create a situation that is so close to dreaming as cinematography when it is at its best. Think only of the time gap: you can make things as long as you want, exactly as in a dream; you can make things as short as you want, exactly as in a dream. As a director, a creator of the picture, you are like a dreamer: you can make what you want, you can construct everything. I think that is one of the most fascinating things that exists.

I think also the reception for the audience of a picture is very, very hypnotic. You sit there in a completely dark room, anonymous, and you look at a lightened spot in front of you and you don't move. You sit and you don't move and your eyes are concentrated on that white spot on the wall. That is some sort of magic. I think it's also magic that two times every frame comes and stands still for twenty-four parts of a second and then it darkens two times; a half part of the time when you see a picture you sit in complete darkness. Isn't that fascinating? That is magic. It's quite different when you watch the television: you sit at home, you have light around you, you have people you know around you, the telephone is ringing, you can go out and have a cup of coffee, the children are making noise, I don't know what—but it is absolutely another situation.

We are in the position to work with the most fascinating medium that exists in the world because like music we go straight to the feeling—not over the intellect—we go straight to the feeling, as in music. Afterward we can start to work with our intellect. If the picture is good, if the suggestions from the creator of the picture are strong enough, they'll give you thoughts afterward; you'll start to think; they are intellectually stimulating.

After you have written a script, do you continue to develop the characters during the shooting?

BERGMAN: No. You know, I have always worked with trained actors; I have never worked with amateurs. An amateur can be himself always and you can put him in situations that give the situation a third dimension, as Vittorio De Sica did in *The Bicycle Thief* [a 1947 classic of Italian "neorealism"], but if you work with trained actors you must know exactly what you are going to do with the parts. We make all the discussions before and then we work in the studio, giving each other suggestions. But the whole time we must have in mind what we meant. And it's very dangerous to go away and suddenly start to improvise. You can improvise, of course, in the studio, but if you improvise you have to be very prepared, because to improvise on an improvisation is always shit. If you are very prepared and know how to do it, you can go back if your improvisation suddenly one day fades away, which it does. Of course it does. Inspiration, enthusiasm, everything like that is beautiful, but I don't like it. When we are in the studio we have to be very strict.

How have you found financing for your films?

BERGMAN: You know, it has never been a real problem for me. Compared to the American or international productions, my pictures are always low-budget productions. *Cries and Whispers* cost about $450,000. *Scenes from a Marriage* cost us about $200,000.

There is always some fool who wants to raise the money. There must be gamblers and optimistic people in the business. Don't you think so?

Could you have made the kinds of films that you make if you were working in America?

BERGMAN: Absolutely not. I think it would have been impossible. I came to the business during the war, in 1942, and Sweden was isolated completely. We could only get German pictures and we didn't want them, so we had to make our pictures ourselves. This was before the TV, so the Swedes were running to the movie theaters very much. This little country with only 7 million people made about forty or fifty pictures a year, so suddenly everybody who knew the front and the back of a camera was a cameraman, and everybody who had ever spoken to an actor was a director.

Of course, it was fantastic, because in three years I had made three pictures, three catastrophes, three flops, and I was still alive. So we could just go on and make films and that was very healthy and unneurotic. It was not a question of making money or making box-office success or something. But when I had made my fifth box-office catastrophe I was kicked out.

I remember the morning when I was kicked out—it was after a catastrophic opening of a picture of mine—I was in bed and I was crying, saying to my girlfriend, "Oh, I think they will never let me make a picture again," and the telephone rang. It was a crazy man who said, "Ingmar, I think you are a little bit more modest now, so perhaps we can work together." And I was. That was the beginning. I am still grateful to that man. He taught me almost everything about filmmaking, because I was a happy amateur, very enthusiastic, and had enormous ideas about making pictures about life and death and everything. Nobody understood my pictures—I don't understand them myself—you know, when I see one of them I get completely red over my whole body. I was a very difficult director. I was very aggressive and I was absolutely terrifying in the studio because I was insecure.

And do you know what the most important thing was that this man taught me? What I still use? You know how it is when we see our dailies; we just say, "God, help me." Isn't it so? Because very often when you see the rushes you have the feeling that you want to go under the bed and never go out again, like a dog.

And we all say, "This is not so bad." Somebody else says, "No, it's pretty good." And then a third says, "It's wonderful." We try to pep ourselves up to have the courage to continue the next day. Well, this man said to me, "I hate this pepping up. Sit, be objective, be your own worst critic. Be cold. Don't let yourself fall down into depression or up into euphoria. Just sit and see it all quietly. Don't blame your crew. All of you have done your best. The only thing you have to ask yourself is, 'Is this all right or do I have to retake it?' Just be objective."

It's almost impossible, but I think that is one of the best things I have learned in my life. And best of all, I think, is to be alone with your God and the projectionist when you see the rushes. Because when people sit there, they are an audience—even if it's a cat, you just sit waiting for something for cats. So it is best of all just to be completely alone.

What is your relation to the camera? Do you feel you have to overcome the technical limitations of the camera?

BERGMAN: If intuition is our mental instrument, the camera is our physical instrument. I think the camera is erotic. It is the most exciting little machine that exists. To me, just to work together with my cameraman, Sven Nykvist, to see a human face with the camera and with a zoom to come closer, to see the scene, to see the face changing, it's the most fascinating thing that exists. The choreography of the actors in relation to the camera is very important. If the actor feels that he is in a good position, in a logical position, he can be with his back to the camera; it doesn't matter. The camera has to be the best friend of the actors, and the actors have to be secure with our handling of the camera. They must feel that we are taking care of them.

Are there many young directors here? Very good. We who are directors must never forget that we are behind the camera and the actor is in front of the camera; he is nude, his soul is nude. If he has confidence in us, we have enormous responsibility. We have something fantastic: we have somebody in our hands and we can destroy him or we can help him in his creative job. To be behind the camera is never difficult, but to be in front of the camera is always a challenge, a difficulty, to be there with your face and your body and all the limitations you have in your soul and all the limitations you feel of your face and your movements, I don't know what. What is strange is that we must not lie to the actors; we have to be absolutely true to them. Better actors like the truth more.

When is the moment you stage the movement or position of camera? When I read the screenplays you write, they always say only what the actors are saying, a bit like a play. When is the moment you state, "The camera will be here"?

BERGMAN: The evening before. When I come home in the evening I just sit down with the script and I read the next day's schedule very carefully. Then I make up my mind about it and I just note the choreography of the actors and the camera. And then in the early morning when I meet Sven—you know, we have worked so many years together—we just very shortly, in five minutes, go through the scene, and I tell him about my ideas for different positions of the camera and the different positions of the actors and the atmosphere of the whole scene. Then we can go on the whole day; it is not necessary to have any discussions. He is a marvelous man. He is very silent and very shy. He is nice. And suddenly everything is there—without any complications—and I can look in the camera and everything I wanted is there.

Do you rehearse with the actors on the set before you plan your shots?

BERGMAN: No, never. That is a very good question. Because if you rehearse with trained actors they go from the mood of intuition to what they are trained to, to stage acting every evening. It's very difficult. If you go on rehearsing with the actors too much, more than just to learn their lessons, and if you rehearse with them several days, some new process in the actors' minds starts. An intellectual process, I think, and that process can be very good, but it's very dangerous for filming because you have something in his eyes suddenly, some sort of "Now I do that" and "I do that" and "I do that." He's conscious of what he's doing. He has to do it intuitively.

Along those same lines, can you tell some of the similarities and differences in working in the theater and the cinema?

BERGMAN: Oh, it's absolutely different. Filmmaking is a neurotic job; it's abnormal to every creative process I know. It's some sort of craftsmanship. You must have a lot of physical power to make a picture. We make three minutes of the picture a day; the terrible thing is, they are three minutes of the picture. If you are at the theater you will rehearse—in Sweden we have about ten or twelve weeks of rehearsal—we start slowly at ten-thirty in the morning and then we go on and it's very lousy and you can sit down and relax; everybody feels that "this is not good today but perhaps next Monday or in the middle of next month we will find out." The creative process is natural, unneurotic.

When you are the film director who has written the script yourself, you have to be some sort of Dr. Jekyll and Mr. Hyde, because if Dr. Jekyll has written the script Mr. Hyde has to direct it, and I tell you they don't like each other that well. I think that is a very schizophrenic situation.

In the theater, we are a group of artists who just come together—it's fantastic; we come together in a house that is built for us to work in. Everything is very important: we come there like very effective, efficient children with our books. At ten-thirty a bell rings and we all go to our rehearsal rooms—and then we are there together with Strindberg or Ibsen or Molière or Shakespeare or any other of those old, marvelous gentlemen, with our thoughts, our emotions, and we have the opportunity to go into it and live with it and try to understand the wisdom of the drama that we are working with.

If I had to make a choice—God save me from that—if somebody came to me and said, "Now, Ingmar, you have long enough made film and theater; you have to make your decision," I am sure I would choose the theater. Because in the theater if you grow old and stuffy and dusty you have a lot of experience, and if you can just pronounce your experience in some crazy words the artists will understand you and you will have a wonderful time with them. My teacher in the theater was a director who was eighty-five years old and could hardly speak, but still he made wonderful, enormous, incredible performances because his soul was young. But he was absolutely a physical wreck. You can't be a wreck when you work in the studio. Perhaps you are, but it's dangerous.

When I was a teacher in the dramatic school in Sweden, with the pupils of the first class we started with a discussion of what you need to make theater. On the blackboard we wrote down about a hundred things: stage, actors, tickets, clothes, money, spotlights, footlights, makeup, theater—more than a hundred different things that we thought we needed. And then I said to them, "Now we take away everything that you think is not necessary." And we went on and went on and went on; we even took away the director. And three things remained. What do you think they were? *Actors.*

BERGMAN: An actor, yes, that's true.

An empty place. A stage.

BERGMAN: It's not necessary.

A script.

BERGMAN: A manuscript, yes. A message. We could call it a message, don't you think so? Two. And a third?

An audience.

BERGMAN: An audience, yes. The class wasn't sure that the audience was necessary, but I thought it was absolutely necessary. And that is my theology about theater: what we need are actors, a message, and an audience. If we have those three things we have a performance. Because the performance is not here on the stage; it is in the hearts of the audience. It is very important to know that. In filmmaking we can learn a lot from the theater, because what we need to make a picture is just that little fantastic machine, the camera, and some film, the negative. That is all.

Just before you start filming, when you get to the set, you said you know as little about the film as the actors do.

BERGMAN: But remember, I have written the script. I have lived with this script perhaps for one or two years. The preparation for the next day, in details, I wait with it as long as possible. Of course, when I made *The Magic Flute* [his film of Mozart's opera] we had to prepare everything before.

You use women as your main characters quite a lot, and I was wondering how you relate to them, how you identify with them? Your male characters aren't very much in the foreground.

BERGMAN: I like more to work with women. I have many good friends who are actors and I like tremendously to work together with them, but in filmmaking it's a job for good nerves and I think the women have much better nerves than men have. It's so. I think the problems very often are the common problems. They are not, on the first hand, women; they are human beings. And God forgive me, but I have the feeling that the prima donnas always are male. I think it has to do with our whole social life and the male part and the female part that they have to play, and it's very difficult to be an actor; it's not so difficult to be an actress in our society.

Would you just talk a little more about what you say to an actor? Do you do exercises with them?

BERGMAN: No, no, no, no. Good heavens, no. I say nothing. I promise.

Do you tell them the message of the film?

BERGMAN: No, good heavens, no. No, no, no, no. I don't know anything about messages or symbols or things like that. Sometimes when I have the message everything goes wrong. So we don't talk about those things. We just talk professionally: "Be careful. Be slower. Don't be in a hurry. Listen." You know, the most important of all is the ear—the ear for the director and the ear for the actors. Listen to each other. Very often when I see a scene I just close my eyes and listen, because if it sounds right it also looks right. It's very strange.

Now we have only a minute to conclude this, to me, wonderful meeting, but I wanted just to add something. Perhaps it sounds like an old uncle, but I am, so it doesn't matter. May I give you an advice?

Yes, please.

BERGMAN: It is a relief to me to know that if I have an intention, if I have a passion and an obsession, if I want to tell somebody something and if I want to touch somebody, the film helps me. But if I have nothing to say and I just want to make a film, I don't make the film. It's so stimulating, the craftsmanship of filmmaking is so terribly stimulating, dangerous, and obsessing, so you can be very tempted . . . but if you have nothing to come with, try to be honest with yourself and don't make the picture. If you have something to come with, if you have emotion and passion, a picture in your head, a tension—even if you aren't very technical—the strange thing is that having worked on the script and having worked with the camera for days and days, suddenly when you have cut it together, the thing you wanted to tell is there.

I have a very good example, Antonioni's *L'Avventura* [Italy, 1960]. The picture is a mess—he had no idea where to put the camera; he had no money; the actors went away; I think he had enormous problems the whole time—but he wanted to tell us something about the loneliness of the human being, and I can see this picture time after time and I don't know what touches me most: how he succeeds without knowing how to do it or what he wants to say. That is very important; that is the most important of all. You have to have something to come with, to give other people.

Picturemaking is some sort of responsibility, that is what I think.

Billy Wilder and I.A.L. Diamond

Billy Wilder and I.A.L. Diamond are among the few enduringly successful marriages of Hollywood writer and director. They have worked together since 1957, an unbroken partnership encompassing twelve of the wittiest and most sophisticated comedy-dramas in the American cinema.

Both were born in Europe, Wilder in Austria in 1906 and Diamond in Rumania in 1920. Wilder, a journalist in Vienna and Berlin, wrote more than a dozen films in Germany, including *Menschem am Sontag (People on Sunday)* and *Emil und die Detektive (Emil and the Detectives)* before fleeing the Nazi tyranny in 1933. He co-directed a film in Paris, *Mauvaise Graine (Bad Seed)* in 1934, and then came to the United States, where he teamed successfully with writer Charles Brackett on several films, including Ernst Lubitsch's *Bluebeard's Eighth Wife* and *Ninotchka*.

Wilder made his American directing debut in 1942 with *The Major and the Minor,* following it with such films as *Double In-*

demnity, The Lost Weekend, A Foreign Affair, and *Sunset Boulevard,* all co-written with Brackett. After making *Ace in the Hole, Stalag 17,* and *Sabrina* with other collaborators, Wilder discovered Diamond's work in a Writers Guild show.

Born Itek Diamond, Wilder's future collaborator was a youthful mathematics genius. He adopted the initials "I.A.L." after winning a competition sponsored by the International Algebraic League. Diamond's comedy skits at Columbia University led to a junior-writer stint in Hollywood, and he became a proficient comedy scenarist on such films as *Two Guys from Milwaukee, Two Guys from Texas, The Girl from Jones Beach,* and Howard Hawks's *Monkey Business.*

Diamond and Wilder began their writing partnership with *Love in the Afternoon* in 1957. Their subsequent films include the classic farce *Some Like It Hot* as well as *The Apartment; Irma la Douce; Kiss Me, Stupid; The Fortune Cookie; The Private Life of Sherlock Holmes; Avanti!; Fedora;* and *Buddy Buddy.* Apart from Wilder, Diamond has written the screenplays of *Merry Andrew, Forty Carats,* and *Cactus Flower.* Together they won the Academy Award for writing *The Apartment* and received the Writers Guild's Laurel Award for Lifetime Achievement, which Wilder had also won with Charles Brackett.

JOINT FILMOGRAPHY

1957 *Love in the Afternoon*   1958 *Some Like It Hot*   1960 *The Apartment*   1961 *One, Two, Three*   1963 *Irma la Douce*   1964 *Kiss Me, Stupid*   1966 *The Fortune Cookie*   1970 *The Private Life of Sherlock Holmes*   1972 *Avanti!*   1974 *The Front Page* 1977 *Fedora*   1981 *Buddy Buddy*

THE SEMINAR

Billy Wilder and I.A.L. Diamond held a seminar with the Fellows of the Center for Advanced Film Studies on January 7, 1976; Wilder also held a seminar on December 13, 1978.

The relation of the writer to the director is often obscure for us as we listen to a director and then to a writer. How do you work together?

WILDER: I'm already very gratified if anybody asks that question, because most people think the actors make up the words. In our case it's very prosaic. We meet at nine-thirty in the morning and open shop like bank tellers. We read *Hollywood Reporter* and *Variety*, exchange the trades, and then we just stare at each other. Sometimes nothing happens. Sometimes it just goes on until twelve-thirty, and then I'll ask him, "How about a drink?" And he nods, and we have a drink and go to lunch. Or sometimes we come full of ideas. This is not the muses coming through the window and kissing our brows; it's very hard work, and having done both, I tell you that directing is a pleasure and writing is a drag.

Directing is a pleasure because you have something to work with: you can put the camera here or there; you can interpret the scene this way or that way. But writing is just an empty page; you start with nothing, absolutely nothing, and, as a rule, writers are vastly underrated and underpaid. It is totally impossible to make a great picture out of a lousy script; it is impossible, on the other hand, for a mediocre director to screw up a great script altogether.

DIAMOND: A writer named Hal Kanter once wrote a monologue for Groucho Marx which had the following line: "Who needs writers? Give me a competent director and two intelligent actors and at the end of eight weeks I will show you three of the most nervous people you ever saw."

Is your way of working normal for writers and directors?

WILDER: I think it is rather abnormal, because from the day we sit down to start working on the screenplay until the time the picture is reviewed by Mr. Canby in New York, we spend all the time together.

DIAMOND: In a normal course of events, if you sell a story or are assigned to a story, you would work first with a producer, and only when he was satisfied would the director come in. If the director is also the producer, then you would skip that middle step; you would be working with him right from the beginning. If he's also a writer, then it depends whether it's a direct collaboration or he just advises you.

Could you take one of your films that were originals, such as The Apartment, *and trace the development of the story?*

WILDER: I saw a picture of David Lean's called *Brief Encounter* [Great Britain, 1946], which was based on a one-act play by Noël Coward. Trevor Howard was the leading man, a married man who has an affair with a married woman, and he uses the apartment of a chum for sexual purposes. I always had it in the back of my mind that the friend of Trevor Howard's who just appears in one or two tiny scenes—who comes back home and climbs into the warm bed the lovers have just left—would make a very interesting character. I made some notes, and years later, after we had finished *Some Like It Hot*, we wanted to make another picture with Jack Lemmon, and I dug this thing out.

DIAMOND: We had the character and the situation but we didn't have a plot until there was a local scandal here where an agent [Jennings Lang] who was having an affair with a client [actress Joan Bennett] was shot by the woman's husband [producer Walter Wanger]. The interesting thing was that he [Lang] was using the apartment of one of the underlings at the agency [MCA], and that was what gave us that relationship—somebody who was using somebody lower than he in a big company, using his apartment.

WILDER: We did not go to this gentleman to produce the picture [Lang did produce Wilder and Diamond's 1974 film, *The Front Page*]. For those days it was a very, very risqué project. Today, of course, it would be considered a Disney picture.

DIAMOND: I also remember some construction problems. There was one point in the second act where Billy said, "The construction is humpbacked"—that is, we were faced with two "exposure" scenes back to back. There was one scene where Fred MacMurray's secretary gives away to his wife that he was having an affair, immediately followed by a scene where the guy who had been thrown out of the apartment gives away to the girl's brother-in-law that she's staying with Lemmon. Billy kept saying, "It's hump-backed; it's humpbacked," but it was the only way we could arrive economically at the third act, so we were just stuck with that construction.

WILDER: But nobody notices that anymore, because neat constructions are out; third acts are out; payoffs are out. Jokes don't have toppers; they just have an interesting straight line and let the audience write their own toppers. We come from a whole different school. The idea that people can sit around a campfire and break wind [in Mel Brooks's *Blazing Saddles*] and people scream for fifteen minutes—that is very strange to us.

DIAMOND: Everybody in this room, I am sure, can quote half a dozen good lines from *Casablanca,* from *Ninotchka,* from *The Maltese Falcon,* and any number of other pictures. The two big laughs in *Shampoo* were: "I want to suck his cock" and "Do you want to fuck?" I think this is hardly a substitute for wit, and it doesn't put very much of a premium on writing clever dialogue.

WILDER: I'm kind of surprised that you used such language—

DIAMOND: I'm just quoting.

Mr. Wilder, what is your role as producer?

WILDER: I just have the final say as far as the making of the picture is concerned, the cutting of the picture and the casting and whatever. My primary role of being a producer is that there is one less nose sticking in my pie. In the old days, and there are still some, there were what you would call creative producers—Selznick, Goldwyn, Thalberg, and now, I imagine, Bob Evans. But usually nowadays a producer is a man who knew a second cousin of a reader who had gotten hold of an unfinished script at Random House about a big fish off Long Island, and for some reason or another his brother-in-law gave him $10,000 and suddenly he has the rights for *Jaws,* and owning that he becomes a producer. But that is not producing.

So what I'm trying to say to you is, if any of you start out and say "I would like to be a producer," no such profession really exists. Most producers make you feel that if they weren't quite that busy and not involved in six enormous projects which were going to revolutionize the cinema, they could write it better, they could direct it better, they could compose, they could possibly act in it.

The truth is that if they can't write it, they can't direct it, they don't know how to write a note of music, they can't act, if they can't do anything, then they become the head of the whole thing. *When you are writing, how detailed is your treatment before you start writing the dialogue?*

WILDER: There is no treatment; we just start right off. And since we are on the stage all the time, when we put it on paper there is no "Slow fade-in; camera tiptoes"—none of that. Just "Day" or "Night"; not even "Morning" or "Evening." We cut through all of that crap, and just the dialogue and whatever jokes or visual gags we have are written down, but none of those fancy descriptions.

I find that young writers, some with very good ideas, get lost, unnecessarily so, in technical descriptions of which they know very little. Nobody will say, "This is a great screenwriter because he always has the camera angles." No. Just have good characters and good scenes and something that plays. The camera technique, that is secondary. That will automatically be fine. But what is the plot? What is the theme? Are we concerned with what is happening? Do we care?

DIAMOND: Most young directors today, if you offered them the choice between a good script and a zoom lens, they'd take the zoom lens.

WILDER: Take away the zoom lens. Just don't let them have it.

DIAMOND: I think it was Penelope Gilliat who said, a few years ago, "Movies have now reached the same stage as sex: it's all technique and no feeling."

WILDER: She was speaking for herself, I'm sure.

I have a question for both of you. Have you ever collaborated in any way in the direction?

WILDER: Oh, he collaborates with me all the time. He just doesn't get the credit for it.

DIAMOND: No, there is no such thing. I will give you an example of two people who used to direct together. Norman Panama and Mel Frank worked as a team, co-directing pictures [Panama and Frank's seven films as co-directors from 1950 through 1956 included *Strictly Dishonorable* and *The Court Jester*], but they had a rule: only one of them was the talking director; only one of them was allowed to talk to the actors. They might consult on the sidelines but always it's one man in charge. No, we don't co-direct. I may sit on the sidelines, and I may make a suggestion occasionally, but I stay out.

Do you have any ambition to direct?

DIAMOND: Not really.

WILDER: If they gave you a zoom lens? Not terribly, because he is a very elegant man and he just does not want to get that close to actors. I have to go into the cage, you know, and he's outside.

How do you work with a cameraman?

WILDER: You have to have a cameraman who has read the script. You will laugh about it, but believe me, you have to ask "Did you read the script?" and not just "Where do you want to put the Kodak?" You make sure that you work with somebody who is as concerned about the outcome of the venture as you are; that he's intelligent; and slowly you begin to speak the same language. You yourself have to be clear in what you want and clear as to how you explain it. It's just madness that has now broken out about the goddamn photography. Everybody wants to photograph better than Sven Nykvist. And they are spending six days waiting for the right sunset. Nobody says that you should photograph it badly, but suddenly it became such a big thing. A sunset is a sunset. Story, story, what's the story?

DIAMOND: In *Alice Doesn't Live Here Any More,* Martin Scorsese, who has a very busy camera, has one scene where two people are sitting in a booth in a restaurant talking to each other. The camera goes 180 degrees to the right, then it comes back 135 degrees to the left, then it goes 90 degrees to the right—none of this for any reason at all except he didn't trust the words in the scene.

WILDER: One of the best scenes I've ever seen in a picture was between Brando and Rod Steiger in *On the Waterfront* [directed by Elia Kazan, 1954], where they are sitting in a cab—not even a transparency [rear-projection screen of a street] in back; they didn't have it, they wanted to save money; instead they had Venetian blinds on the window of the cab; nobody cared. The camera was there and the two brothers were talking, especially Brando, beautifully and very well written [by Budd Schulberg]. It was a scene that lasted seven minutes, no cut, no close-ups, no nothing;

one of the great scenes, because you were involved. But I'm not going to like the scene any better if they suddenly get up and walk out there.

DIAMOND: The tipoff is usually in the middle of a scene: somebody says, "Let's get some air."

WILDER: I ran into Scorsese on New Year's Eve. He just did another new picture which is very good called *Taxi Driver*, and he was talking about simplifying, simplifying. He knows that; he learned it; it's just that with a young colt, you have to put the blinkers on him. But he's going to calm down. He's going to be fine. He's a very fine talent, Scorsese is. I don't want you to have a feeling just because I'm a veteran elderly director that I think we made better than they make now. They make terrific pictures. We have young directors now who are better than anything we had. I think Hal Ashby is very fine. Bertolucci is marvelous. I think Coppola's *Godfather II* is certainly among the five best American pictures ever made. On my list of the unforgettable ones it's way up there with Renoir's *Grand Illusion*, Wyler's *Best Years of Our Lives*, Lean's *Bridge on the River Kwai*, Huston's *Maltese Falcon*, Ford's *The Informer*, and some of the old German pictures, the Murnau pictures. [F. W. Murnau's German films included *Nosferatu* and *The Last Laugh*.] For a man who had made only four or five pictures, *Godfather II* was an outstanding achievement, a very mature work of a very mature man.

You were saying earlier that you felt writers were underrated and underpaid, and Mr. Diamond was also saying that there was a trend away from respect for good writing. I was wondering if you had any suggestions for improving the situation.

DIAMOND: I think there's probably more respect for writing today than at any other time in the history of the industry.

WILDER: Absolutely.

DIAMOND: On the other hand, I see something else happening, which is that not that many people are interested in just writing anymore; they see it as a stepping-stone toward directing. This is as if every composer said to himself, "It's Bernstein and Previn who get the publicity; if I can just knock off a piece maybe they'll let me conduct it." But it is a discipline in itself. It may have something to do with directing and it may not. But as I say, I find too many, certainly the younger kids, who are primarily interested in directing, because, let's face it, that's the big ego trip; there's more recognition for the director than the writer. And I hate to see that happen because there are never enough good writers.

Financially, the writer is in a very strong position today, because in the old days you could not sell an original screenplay unless it was for a Western at Republic [a studio, now defunct, that specialized in low-budget formula Westerns]. It was all either books or plays or scripts written by contract writers at the studios. A good original screenplay can now command tremendous sums of money, and I think it is more wide open than it ever was before.

WILDER: My suggestion is that you cannot just freelance and hop around town; you have to latch onto a director with whom you work most of the time or, preferably, continuously. There is an understanding, right? But it's tougher, believe me, to get on with a collaborator on a script, or in a director-writer relationship, than in one's marriage. But if you find the proper director, he's got respect for you and you've got respect for him. Somebody asked me one day, "Is it important for a director to know how to write?" It's not important; it's important for a director to know how to *read*. You may laugh, but it's very difficult. So when you find a director who knows how to read, who asks the proper questions, who is not ashamed to say "I don't get the meaning of this scene," instead of just pooh-poohing the thing and shooting something which is contrary to what you wanted to express in that scene—if you find it's simpatico with a director, hold on: And if you're good I'm sure he will hold on to you, because good writers are rare.

Have you ever found yourself on a set improvising dialogue, or the whole scene?

DIAMOND: Never, never, never. If you ever listen to actors talk, you will not improvise.

WILDER: We should have, maybe. Totally improvise, no, but sometimes we sense that it does not work, and we withdraw into a corner and rewrite a little or do something during lunchtime. But to sit there for half a day and then kind of slap it together, no, never.

DIAMOND: The real improviser is the writer, because by the time you've gotten to shooting a scene he may have written it fifteen different ways. The stuff that goes into the wastebasket is improvisation. That's obviously much more economical than waiting until you get on the set with electricians standing around to start to improvise. You have to make the decision that this is the way you're going, and if you start to screw around with one scene, obviously it affects every other scene in the script. Now, Altman may shoot an eight-hour picture like *Nashville* and cut it down to two and a half hours, but this is not the normal way to make pictures, and it's not a very feasible way.

WILDER: I remember distinctly now the moment when I decided to become a director. This was forty-five years ago. It was when I saw a picture I had written in Germany for the old UFA company [the leading German film studio of the 1920s]. There was some kind of nightclub in the picture with a big sign outside: "Shoes and ties obligatory." There were two doormen, and they were looking to see that the people were wearing shoes and ties. So, one of the gags I wrote in there was that a man had a long beard, right? And the doorman stops him and looks under the beard to see if the guy has a tie. Now I go see the picture: the director gave that actor a little Van Dyke. There was nothing to lift and look under. He kept that joke in there because he thought it was still going to be funny, but it was not. So I just said, "Well." But can you imagine how much they miss now?

DIAMOND: I once wrote a scene that took place in the Guggenheim Museum, and at the time I was writing it I had no idea what the exhibit would be when we finally got around to shooting it, so I just said, "It's an op art show, and two characters are standing in front of a geometric painting, and one says to the other, 'I bet he cheated and used a ruler.'" Just a throwaway line to get the scene started. They get there six months later, and you see somebody standing in front of a piece of round sculpture, and the line is, "I bet he cheated and used a ruler." It occurred to nobody on the set—the director, the actor, the script girl—that somebody should have said, "Wait a minute, this line is wrong now. We either have to change it or throw it out altogether." But this is where sometimes people will stick too literally to the script.

WILDER: It is respect for the written word, and you should be very proud.

Have you ever had the experience that you've written something, you've gone to direct it, but it's gone flat on you and you haven't had the freshness or perspective to fix it?

WILDER: Most of the time, six out of eight times, but you just have to go. You designed the plane; you took off; you thought it was going to soar; now you're in the plane and it just kind of stalls, so you just try to get to your destination or it's going to crash on you. You try to do the best you can. You just don't know. If it happens to be a play and you're trying it out in Pittsburgh, you can rewrite it, and if that does not work you just don't bring it to New York. We don't bury our dead. And it's going to stink years from now on television, it's going to pursue us, and it's absolutely awful. But if you bat four out of ten, terrific, better than Mickey Mantle, a well-known director.

In your visual style you very often seem to concentrate on one particular object. Is that usually in the script?

WILDER: Sure. When we constructed *The Apartment*, we knew we needed a scene in which Mr. Lemmon realizes that Shirley MacLaine is the dame his boss, Mr. MacMurray, does it to in his apartment, a realization scene, right? So we go back and plant the little makeup mirror that she has in the apartment. Ultimately, when Lemmon buys himself the young-executive black bowler and she says, "You look fine" and shows him in the mirror, then he suddenly realizes "That's the girl." So we may go back, but surely none of those things is improvised; it's all calculated and planted.

I've seen Some Like It Hot *about half a dozen times, and I know what's coming but I always laugh. How did you manage to pull off having two men dress up as women?*

WILDER: Very early on my friend Mr. Diamond very rightly said—and this was the most important thing in the structure of the picture—"We have to find the hammerlock; we have to find the ironclad thing where those two guys trapped in women's clothes cannot just take the wigs off and say, 'Look, I'm a guy.' It has to be a question of life and death." And that's where the idea of the Valentine's Day murders came in, where if they got out of the women's clothes they would be killed by the Al Capone gang or whoever it was. And I remember, when we started working on the picture I had a discussion with David O. Selznick, who was a very fine producer. I told him the plot very briefly, and he said, "You mean there's going to be machine guns and shooting and killing and blood?" I said, "Yeah, sure." He said, "It's not going to be funny. No comedy can survive that kind of brutal reality." But that's what made the picture. They were on the spot and we kept them on the spot until the very end.

How has the relaxation of censorship on screen affected your work?

WILDER: Well, one can tackle more daring themes, and one can write dialogue without that straitjacket; it used to be that if you wanted to call someone a son of a bitch you would have to say, "If he had a mother she'd bark." More people in the Army said "Darn you" and all of that. But I don't think we would ever write an out-and-out porno picture.

DIAMOND: Especially in comedy, it's almost gratuitous. I think nudity hurts laughs. I mean, if you're watching somebody's boobs you're not listening to the dialogue. I don't think *The Philadelphia Story* would be any better or funnier if you saw Cary Grant and Katharine Hepburn in the nude.

WILDER: Hepburn? Big laugh. *Shampoo* had an absolutely marvelous idea, the ambulatory hairdresser with the penis hairdryer under his belt, chugging around Beverly Hills, and it had those couple of dirty lines, you know. But I personally would be embarrassed to go to Julie Christie and say, "Here's the dialogue for tomorrow." I would run and hide somewhere. Ernst Lubitsch's pictures were never censorable, but they were much more erotic than any of the pictures made now. You had to be clever. There are times when I wish we had censorship, because the fun has gone out of it, the game that you played with them.

But I do respect a director such as William Friedkin, who suddenly is confronted with a scene in *The Exorcist* such as a party going on and the eight-year-old girl joins the party and pees on the carpet. That's just a day's work, right? Where do you put the camera? It is not easy. I can do a chase sequence; I can do any goddamned thing; but an eight-year-old girl peeing during a party, that's a new one. It requires a different technique. But it is this kind of never-seen-before that makes for enormous box office. I think that once you make up your mind to do a picture like this, you've got to give it both knees, because it is not going to be in great taste and very subtle. If you do it, then do it. That's Sam Peckinpah's technique, the man who gives it three knees.

What are you working on now?

WILDER: We very probably will retire, like Secretariat, to stud. No, we'll do something, but it's like this gentleman said, you get a little scared. Is it pertinent enough? Is it new enough? Is it big enough? Who are we going to have in there? Just another picture —that doesn't interest us. You hope that the game will go into an extra inning, because you feel you've still got a few hits left. And if that does not work, I'm just going to sign up with a Japanese team and sit on the bench and wait for Kurosawa to break his leg.

THE ACTOR
Sidney Poitier

One of the finest actors of his time, and one of the most successful actor-directors in Hollywood, Sidney Poitier was also a trailblazer for the neglected black minority in American films. He was the first black to achieve full-fledged star status in Hollywood, as well as the first to win the Academy Award for best actor.

When Poitier made his first Hollywood film in 1949, blacks were still mostly relegated to playing caricatured menials or comic types. Poitier changed all that with his strong and dignified portrayals of black men who were also doctors, lawyers, teachers, police officers, writers—roles of social respect that won him the praise of Dr. Martin Luther King Jr. for carving "an imperishable niche in the annals of our nation's history."

Born in 1927 in Miami, Florida, to a family of farmers, Poitier was raised on Cat Island in the Bahamas. With only eighteen months of formal education, he became an actor after moving to New York at the age of eighteen and working in a number of menial jobs. His stage role in *Anna Lucasta* led to an offer from Darryl F. Zanuck of 20th Century-Fox to play a doctor in a film about bigotry, *No Way Out*. Poitier quickly established himself as a star with such groundbreaking '50s films as *Cry, the Beloved*

Country; *The Blackboard Jungle*; *Edge of the City*; *The Defiant Ones*; and *Raisin in the Sun*.

Poitier won his Oscar for *Lilies of the Field* in 1963, and his popularity peaked in 1967, when he appeared in *To Sir with Love, In the Heat of the Night*, and *Guess Who's Coming to Dinner*. In his personal life he was active in the civil rights movement, but the rise of black militancy led to his displacement as a cinematic role model by a new generation of angrier black actors. He became a figure of controversy, and he eventually turned his sights more to producing and directing.

His first production was *Brother John* in 1971, and he made his directing debut the following year with a Western, *Buck and the Preacher*. Since then he has directed six more films, including the 1980 Richard Pryor–Gene Wilder comedy hit, *Stir Crazy*, and three highly successful comedies starring himself and Bill Cosby: *Uptown Saturday Night, Let's Do It Again*, and *A Piece of the Action*. Poitier published his autobiography, *This Life*, in 1980. He was founding vice-chairman of the AFI.

FILMOGRAPHY

1949 *From Whom Cometh My Help*   1950 *No Way Out*   1952 *Cry, the Beloved Country* / *Red Ball Express*   1954 *Go, Man, Go!*   1955 *The Blackboard Jungle*   1956 *Goodbye, My Lady*   1957 *Edge of the City* / *Something of Value* / *Band of Angels*   1958 *Mark of the Hawk* / *The Defiant Ones* / *The Virgin Island*   1959 *Porgy and Bess*   1960 *All the Young Men*   1961 *Raisin in the Sun* / *Paris Blues*   1962 *Pressure Point*   1963 *Lilies of the Field*   1964 *The Long Ships*   1965 *The Greatest Story Ever Told* / *The Bedford Incident* / *A Patch of Blue*   1966 *The Slender Thread* / *Duel at Diablo*   1967 *To Sir with Love* / *In the Heat of the Night* / *Guess Who's Coming to Dinner*   1968 *For Love of Ivy*   1969 *The Lost Man*   1970 *They Call Me Mister Tibbs!*   1971 *The Organization* / *Brother John*   1972 *Buck and the Preacher* (also director)   1973 *A Warm December* (also director)   1974 *Uptown Saturday Night* (also director)   1975 *The Wilby Conspiracy* / *Let's Do It Again* (also director)   1977 *A Piece of the Action* (also director)   1980 *Stir Crazy* (director only)   1982 *Hanky Panky* (director only)

THE SEMINAR

Sidney Poitier held a seminar with the Fellows of the Center for Advanced Film Studies on January 28, 1976.

What gave you the desire to go behind the camera?
POITIER: I went into directing to add some longevity to my career in the business, not necessarily as an actor. I shall be fifty quite soon; I had felt impotent for a long time, just waiting by a telephone for my next job. My career cannot go on into perpetuity by my sitting at the phone. Therefore, I had to create some activity for myself. That's why I went into directing; I didn't go into directing because I had an overwhelming desire to displace Truffaut or any of the other guys.

I love doing film; I *love* it. If I had to wait for a job, I might work every other year; jobs are not easy to come by. I engineered my last ten jobs. Of the four pictures I've produced, my company produced them. I was in a position to hire myself.

The pictures you have directed so far have been mostly action pictures and comedies [with the exception of the love story A Warm December*], and they have been very successful commercially. Do you have any projects that you know won't make any money but you want to do anyway?*
POITIER: Being a director in this day and age requires a little bit of the entrepreneurial jazz. I would like for all of my pictures to make a few dollars. I will never start out to make a picture that I know is not going to make money. I've made a lot of bombs; I even made a picture that didn't get back its advertising cost. I mean, how important can the comment be? You spend a million to *say* something? Spend a million, have a lot of people come and see it, and *then* make your comment.

If I have something to say in my films, I want to say it to everyone, or to as many people as I can. Now, there are certain pieces of material that just won't necessarily attract a large audience. But you can say pretty much what you want in almost anything. I'm convinced of that.

Several distributors have come through here and said that there is a ceiling on the rentals from films with predominantly black casts, somewhere between $4 million and $5 million. Have you found that to be true?

POITIER: I have two pictures now that together will have rentals of $20 million or $22 million [*Uptown Saturday Night* and *Let's Do It Again*], so that can't be true. There is obviously a problem for the black filmmaker: he has to make the kind of film that will attract beyond the black community. Well, that's not such a big problem, is it? First of all, you've got the opportunity to make films. Having that opportunity, I'm not going to waste my time in picayune evaluations such as $4 million here and $5 million there, and what will the black picture do as opposed to the white picture. I have an audience of hundreds of millions of people around the world. It is up to *me* to reach them. It behooves me to say, "OK, you can get to the black audience with this. If they are satisfied, can you still attract attention elsewhere?" That's a unique problem for the black filmmaker, and I think it spices up his opportunities and his life.

How much input did you have as an actor when you first started making movies, when you were one of the first blacks out here? What was your relationship with the writers and directors as far as your character and the story line were concerned?

POITIER: When I started, the only leverage I had was to refuse to work in that particular script if it had such objectionable portions, or certain comments inherent in it that were antiblack or antihuman or just against my own sense of integrity, my sense of my being as a human entity. I would say, "Thank you, but I cannot work in it because . . ." That was always a last resort. I have always been able to talk to people. What I would do is raise the question of my objections as seductively as I could.

I have never met a producer who was not interested in my concept of the "blackness" of a script. However, "blackness" has changed in concept over the last twenty years, and I have been making films for twenty-six years. What was of particular value to us in terms of our priorities twenty years ago was antiquated five years later; and what was important ten years ago is today quite old hat. So I have to speak in the context of what was at that time. I sought to present as forceful an image as I could, counter to the prevalent one. The prevalent image in those days was that the niggers were lazy, shiftless, screw a lot. So, in my pictures, I was cool, hardworking—I did a lot of screwing, but not in the pictures.

Seriously, though, if you will examine the films, you will see that I tried to present that which was most lacking: a guy with a job other than the ten menials. So I played a lot of doctors, a lot of lawyers; that was *that* time, and it was, to my mind, a very interesting period. Many of those films are certainly heavily dated today, but I believe in the historical evolution of things: you and I are in this room here partly because of that history. I've had job opportunities partly because there were black actors before me who died and never had a shot, you see. I am here partly because of the dues they paid—and I am talking about Frank Wilson, Canada Lee, Rex Ingram, Hattie McDaniel, Louise Beavers, all those guys. So my little stint was not unrelated to theirs, you follow? As yours will certainly not be unrelated to mine. In the evolutionary concept, in terms of the total, we have come from there to here; and, if you will examine it, you will see that I existed at a certain point, and, to succeed me, will be that group and that group and that group as we go on. I succeeded Canada Lee, and Canada Lee succeeded guys like Paul Robeson. You go farther back, and you get all the way back to Ira Aldrich.

When I was growing up, you were the only black male image that I had to relate to on the screen. Now you are one of the premier black actors, if not the premier black actor. Other people came along at the same time you did—Harry Belafonte, Moses Gunn, Brock Peters, and people like that. Why do you think they were not able to make it in the film world, and you were?

POITIER: There are many things that go into that. First of all, there was a quotient of luck that we can't really measure, so we dispense with that. There were other things going for me. Actors have a certain kind of energy, and that energy translates itself in the way people receive you on the screen. There are some actors who are destined to be character actors, supporting actors, and there are some actors whose skills are not necessarily gargantuan but who have energy—some people call it force, some call it presence—and that energy, with other externals, helps to produce a certain longevity. I think that's what happened in my case. I can't lay claim to having done it myself; there were too many externals. But I think that explains why a good number of other guys haven't—yet.

I came to California for the first time to do a film in 1949. During that period they would say, "We're looking for a black actor." And old Sidney, he was young and he was tall and he was nice and he spoke kind of nicely and he moved not too badly, and when he smiled, he was friendly. Now, you see, James Earl Jones couldn't have done it at that time. James Earl Jones's power and energy were phenomenal, but the times were not ready for that, as the times were not ready earlier for Robeson and Canada.

What in your childhood caused you to go into acting?

POITIER: I was a very peculiar child. I came from a very large family, but it was not what we would call a closely knit family today. I grew up on Cat Island in the Bahamas, and there were no automobiles and no protective mechanism necessary for a child growing up except to teach him to swim before he could walk. We lived very near an ocean, and before I could walk I was taught how to swim. Once I could swim, nobody paid me any attention anymore, because there was nothing you could do to get into trouble—if you fell in, you could climb out. So I grew up alone a lot. I grew up before I was prepared for it, and had the captainship of my life. I got into being my own best company and I got into an awful lot of daydreaming. As I grew up, the habit-pattern of daydreaming—which later was, I suspect, very helpful to me—armed me with an ability to slip in and out of characters. We moved to a part of the world [Nassau] where there were movies when I was twelve. For those among my family and friends who couldn't go to the movies, I would have to come back and relate to them what I had seen; I enjoyed doing that more than I enjoyed seeing the movies. So a combination of things brought me to film.

I had a sister, who has since passed away, and when I was about thirteen I said to her that I was going to go to Hollywood and become a cowboy. Now, I had no intentions of coming to *this* Hollywood. I supposed that Hollywood was where cowboys were. What I wanted to do was work with cows. I later learned that that was in Texas.

But I think many things conspired. When I was eighteen, in New York, I had no interest, on a conscious level, in theater as such. I didn't know that theater was a thing you could work in. I was a dishwasher. I had just come out of the Army and I was looking for things to do. I was equipped to do nothing but work with my hands. Washing dishes was very cool, because I got my meals. That's dynamite when you live by yourself: two meals a day. I was a transient dishwasher, meaning that I would work one restaurant one day, and I would go back to the employment office and they'd send me to another the next day. I was a relief dishwasher. One day I decided to get a *steady* dishwashing job. In order to do that, I bought a black newspaper in New York called *The Amsterdam News*. They had a marvelous collection of jobs for unskilled workers; over here it said, "Dishwashers, Porters Wanted," and over here it said, "Actors Wanted." Well!

I went over to this place, and there was a man there [Frederick O'Neal] who is, today, a very good friend. I said, "I'm here to apply for this job of one of those actors." And he said, "Oh? Are you an actor?" I said, "Of course." I went up on the stage, and that's the first time I'd opened a script. I went to school for a year and a half in my entire life. I could barely read. So I opened it up, and I said, "Well . . . I . . . am . . . very . . ." I heard the guy slam his script down. He said, "Did you have to come in here and waste my time like this?" Of course, this was while he had me by the scruff of the neck, heading me toward the door. True story. He pushed me out and he said these words: "Why don't you go and get yourself a job as a dishwasher?"

Now, I didn't mind that he had thrown me out. I took a chance, you know. But inherent in what he suggested was a challenge to me. I was then committed, it seems, to pursue a course away from the suggestion. So I went and got a job as a dishwasher, and I earned enough money to start studying acting. I intended to become an actor only to prove—not to him, but to me—that I didn't have to be a dishwasher. That's how I started.
Where did you study?
POITIER: I studied at the American Negro Theater, the very place I was thrown out of. In order to get in there in those days, you took an audition, and they auditioned every six months. There was an exceptionally high percentage of female actors auditioning, and the small percentage of male actors were, as a body, pretty poor. They selected the students they wanted and they found out it was imbalanced—something like eighteen girls, and there were really only three or four guys who showed *anything*. So they had to pad the male side. The pickings were so lean that they took me!

They said they were taking me on a trial basis. After three

months, if the teacher thought I was not improving, they would have to ask me to leave. Well, at the end of three months they asked me to leave. But I wasn't ready to leave. There was a man named Abram Hill, the administrator of the school—Osceola Archer was the artistic director—so I went to Abe Hill and I said, "Mr. Hill, you do not have a janitor for the school after hours. I'll tell you what: I'll be the janitor if you let me stay for another three months." And he snapped me up!

Luck would have it, right? Osceola Archer decided to do a student production called *Days of Our Youth*. There was a dynamite part in it for a young actor. She didn't think I was ready for it, so she hired a young actor by the name of Harry Belafonte. Harry's father was a janitor in Harlem, and Harry used to help his dad on certain evenings. One evening when he was supposed to be at rehearsal, a producer-director by the name of James Light came up to see what Osceola Archer was doing with *Days of Our Youth*. We were waiting for Harry to show up, and everybody got a little restless. Finally they said, "Well, why don't you read Harry's part until he gets here?" Now I've learned a little bit, see? So I read Harry's part. After we ran through it, this guy said to me, "Why don't you come down to my office next week and we'll have a talk?"

I did. He was about to produce a black version of Gilbert Seldes's translation of Aristophanes's *Lysistrata*, and he hired me to play Polydoros, a young soldier. Well, I had twelve lines. Opening night, five minutes before the curtain, I see guys going up and peeking through a tiny little hole in the curtain, and I say, "What the hell is that?" I go up to the curtain and I peek through—and I see *two thousand people*! They're all just sitting there. Well, I get *so* scared. This is my very first job. Finally it comes time for me to go out. I don't want to go. A stagehand finally comes over [demonstrates a shove] and I am out!

The guy throws me his line, right? Instead of answering him with my first line, I give him my ninth line. I can see his eyes rolling in his head. He's going to try and recover, you see, so he shoots me what is normally his second line, and I give him my line, number eight. Well, the audience at that point starts laughing. Now from scared I'm mad. I can't stand people to laugh at me—laugh with me, but not at me. I had too many insecurities at that age.

So he says so-and-so, and I say so-and-so. I still haven't found the right line. I don't know that the audience is laughing at the incongruity of what I'm saying in response to what I'm being asked. They think it's part of the play and they love it. I decide, "That's it—I am not going to stand here and be laughed at," and I walk off the stage. They start applauding! I think they're glad to get rid of me, and that's why they're applauding.

I went up to my dressing room, and I went through a real deep despair, right? I got dressed. This was to be my curtain. This was the end of my theatrical career, right there. I came downstairs and slipped out of the theater and went for a long, long walk. There was a theater party afterward. I didn't want to go. Next day the reviews came out. Uniformly, they destroyed the play. In those days they had eleven critics, and every one of them said: ". . . except that young man who came on in the first act and just devastated everybody with his so-and-so. He had such marvelous charm . . ." Me? Indeed, it was me; they were talking about me. Well, the play lasted three or four nights. Every night I went out there I did it the proper way. I didn't get the big laughs. There was no way for me to re-create that first night, but I felt terrific. I went back to the American Negro Theater and I studied some more. Within a few months I got a job as an understudy in *Anna Lucasta.* I went on the road. That's how it all started.

In the transition from acting to directing, were there any difficulties you hadn't expected?

POITIER: My greatest difficulty came on the very first day I directed. The self-doubt that must be faced came up for me on the first day. I had seen the camera and I knew what it was about, I knew lens sizes, but how to use the camera as an instrument of your own creative process was all new to me. I felt the panic building up in me when I made my first setup. I was scared. Then I began to watch the actors unfold in the frame that I had structured, and they began to make sense. They seemed to be real. What they were doing had some kinship to my view of reality, and I began to relax.

When Truffaut was here, we asked him what difficulties he had in acting and directing at the same time. He said the biggest difficulty was the desire to say "cut" too soon.

POITIER: Well, that wasn't *my* problem. When you are acting in the film you are directing, the consciousness is divided into two areas. I didn't have to spend too much time with my acting. After twenty-six years, much of it becomes second nature. I'm dealing with a new area; I'm dealing with moving actors around; I'm dealing with a sense of what sounds correct and what looks real.

When I had to carry the weight as an actor in a particular sequence, of course, I had to pay much more attention to what I was doing. There are some things I do as an actor that I have to be very careful of: I take too much time. I was trained in the habit of using pauses. Sometimes they're effective and sometimes they're not. As a director, I knew I had this problem, because I had seen some films I had been directed in, and I found that I was guilty of overplaying certain sequences with pauses. So I allowed myself very few pauses, because I was not too sure. I think it takes a touch of schizophrenia to be able to do it well.

We're starting out as directors. What can you say that would help us talk better to the actor?

POITIER: Well, that's very personal. I'll tell you how I deal with actors, having been one for a great many years. Actors are very sensitive instruments, and I will never give an actor instructions that other actors can hear, unless it's a general instruction. I find that if I'm given a specific instruction—and this may be my neurosis as an actor—on the floor, where everybody hears the instruction, then all those people become arbiters as to whether I did or did not fulfill the instruction, which inhibits an actor. It puts an unnecessary restriction on him.

I did a picture some years ago for a director who had the habit of giving instructions very loud and very clear, even the most intimate instructions. I found I couldn't work. So I speak in private, by going up to the actor. If there are two actors involved, I can get them to work in concert without telling one actor what the other guy's instructions are. By so doing, I find that my actors are completely confident. They will try anything, because there are no judges except me and, probably, themselves.

And sometimes you work with actors who, by their particular nature, are nervous people. You have to husband that nervous energy, that adrenalin, very carefully, because if the actor is not secure his automatic response is to withdraw. He will cover his tools; he will put kind of a protective screen between you and him.

What do you see in the future as an employment market for young black talent—actors, directors, and so forth?

POITIER: I would just like to remind you of how fortunate we are, you and me. We have 27 million black Americans who have arrived at a station in their self-awareness that they want to see themselves in film, and they want to see new horizons of themselves in films. There was a time when the forerunners of those people were not necessarily satisfied, but they lived with going to see other people in movies. There was never a time before now when there was a conscious, individual effort to say "I want to see *myself*—in *all* of my dimensions—on film." That is what you have to work with today.

Unfortunately, you've got to deal with the hierarchy of the economic structure in this town. But listen: so you gotta deal with it? Deal with it. Learn your entrepreneurship. I don't care how good a director you are, you've got to put deals together; you've got to make it attractive to the guys you're going to get the money from. If the guys you are going to get the money from are black guys, you will still have to put it all together. And you ain't seen no hard dudes till them!

I respect your hesitation, and I admire your determination. We have a hell of a long way to go, we black people, but don't go too long without realizing that, over the last fifteen years, we've come a hell of a long way. Do you *hear* me? Seventeen years ago, I was there by myself. There was no Gordon Parks Jr., no Michael Schultz, no Jim Brown, no Fred Williamson, no young actors, no young actresses, no assistant directors, no editors. When I first walked on the 20th Century-Fox lot, I was there with the shoeshine boy. There were only two blacks there. I worked at Columbia Pictures when there wasn't another black person to be seen. Today you cannot walk onto a lot without seeing black secretaries, black people who work as assistant directors. I am a believer in history, and where you are now would have been paradise for those who went before us. And it is in that context that I say, "Buck up and go get 'em!"

Lucille Ball

Lucille Ball is one of the great American comediennes. Her enormously popular Lucy shows ran for twenty-three years on CBS-TV, and the original *I Love Lucy* is still running in syndication throughout the world. She was the first film star to make a successful transition to the fledgling television medium; indeed, TV has proved to be her natural element. Her career is further remarkable because she became the first female studio head in Hollywood since Mary Pickford was a partner in United Artists.

Ball and her then-husband, co-star, and Desilu producing partner, Desi Arnaz, pioneered the three-camera TV technique with *I Love Lucy* from 1951 to 1957. With the profits from selling the show's reruns to CBS, they formed their own studio. They bought the RKO lots in Hollywood and Culver City, where Desilu and other producers made more than fifty TV series, including such hits as *The Untouchables, Our Miss Brooks, Mission: Impossible,* and *Star Trek*. After their divorce, Ball became president of the studio in 1962 and won a reputation as a shrewd businesswoman. She sold Desilu to Gulf & Western in 1967 for a profit of more than $10 million.

Born in 1911, Ball began her career as a model and chorus girl in New York City. She went to Hollywood in 1933 as a Goldwyn girl in the chorus of Busby Berkeley's musical *Roman Scandals*, with Eddie Cantor. For several years she served a busy apprenticeship as second banana to the Marx Brothers, Fred Astaire and Ginger Rogers, and even the Three Stooges. Her first notable film role came in 1937, as part of the superb ensemble cast of *Stage Door*, with Katharine Hepburn and Ginger Rogers.

Although she never reached her true potential in films, Ball's unconventional good looks and effervescent personality helped enhance such films as *The Affairs of Annabel, Five Came Back,* Dorothy Arzner's 1940 feminist musical *Dance, Girl, Dance, The Big Street, DuBarry Was a Lady, Miss Grant Takes Richmond,* and *Fancy Pants.*

She has acted in only a few features since her departure for television; her last was *Mame,* in 1974. She married producer Gary Morton in 1961 and is still active on TV specials. In 1976, two years after her third Lucy series went off the air, CBS honored its beloved star with a retrospective special, *CBS Salutes Lucy: The First 25 Years.* Her children, Lucie Arnaz and Desi Jr., have become professional actors.

FILMOGRAPHY

1933 *Broadway Thru a Keyhole / Blood Money / Roman Scandals / The Bowery* 1934 *Moulin Rouge / Nana / Bottoms Up / Hold That Girl / Bulldog Drummond Strikes Back / The Affairs of Cellini / Kid Millions / Broadway Bill / Jealousy / Men of the Night / The Fugitive Lady* 1935 *Carnival / The Whole Town's Talking / Roberta / Old Man Rhythm / The Three Musketeers / Top Hat / I Dream Too Much* 1936 *Chatterbox / The Farmer in the Dell / Follow the Fleet / Bunker Bean/ That Girl from Paris / Winterset* 1937 *Don't Tell the Wife / Stage Door* 1938 *Joy of Living / Go Chase Yourself / Having Wonderful Time / The Affairs of Annabel / Room Service / The Next Time I Marry / Annabel Takes a Tour* 1939 *Beauty for the Asking / Twelve Crowded Hours / Panama Lady / Five Came Back / That's Right—You're Wrong* 1940

The Marines Fly High / *You Can't Fool Your Wife* / *Dance, Girl, Dance* / *Too Many Girls* / 1941 *A Girl, A Guy, and a Gob* / *Look Who's Laughing* 1942 *Valley of the Sun* / *The Big Street* / *Seven Days' Leave* 1943 *DuBarry Was a Lady* / *Best Foot Forward* / *Thousands Cheer* 1944 *Meet the People* 1945 *Without Love* / *Abbott and Costello in Hollywood* 1946 *Ziegfeld Follies* / *The Dark Corner* / *Easy to Wed* / *Two Smart People* / *Lover Come Back* 1947 *Lured* / *Her Husband's Affairs* 1949 *Sorrowful Jones* / *Easy Living* / *Miss Grant Takes Richmond* 1950 *A Woman of Distinction* / *Fancy Pants* / *The Fuller Brush Girl* 1951 *The Magic Carpet* 1954 *The Long, Long Trailer* 1956 *Forever, Darling* 1960 *The Facts of Life* 1963 *Critic's Choice* 1967 *A Guide for the Married Man* 1968 *Yours, Mine, and Ours* 1974 *Mame* 1983 *All the Right Moves* (producer only)

TELEVISION SERIES

1951–1957 *I Love Lucy* 1962–1967 *The Lucy Show* 1968–1974 *Here's Lucy*

THE SEMINAR

Lucille Ball held a seminar with the Fellows of the Center for Advanced Film Studies on January 18, 1974.

You've probably made us laugh more than anyone else in show business.
BALL: I baby-sat for three generations. I'm very proud of that.
As directors sometimes we're going to have to try to get comedy performances from beginners. When little Lucie and Desi Jr. came to your show, what kinds of things did you tell them to make them funnier?
BALL: First of all, it has to be in the writing. They weren't just born funny, although I must say Lucie has a weird, woolly sense of humor. Desi doesn't; he's more the serious type, but when he plays comedy seriously he's great. That's the way comedy should be played.

I reiterate, the words have got to be there. My writers were sensational; they're still with me: Madelyn Pugh Davis and Bob Carroll Jr. I learned from just doing what they wrote. Their directions to me were a page or two pages of what to do and how to do it. They really did it themselves before they asked me to do it, which is unusual.

There's no way to make someone funny. There's no way to tell people about timing. You *can* tell them about listening, and reacting before they act. I don't think a person who never learns to listen and react before he acts can be funny. I'm not saying you can't be taught to do comedy, but you just can't make everyone funny. If you are a director you must be aware that they mustn't ever try to be funny.

It's the way you perform. It's the believability. I had to have a childlike belief in the things that I did, because they were so exaggerated. If I had to bake a loaf of bread that was literally thirteen feet long, I believed it.
What did you learn from Buster Keaton?
BALL: Buster was a personal friend. I never got a chance to work with him, but he was at MGM when I was there. Buster helped me get a marvelous act together, the only act that I did in vaude-

ville. And he taught me about props—fabulous man with props. Props have been so important to me.

You'd be amazed at how many people cannot pick up a prop, let alone work conveyor belts and do the things that Viv [Vivian Vance, her co-star on *I Love Lucy* and *The Lucy Show*] and I did, or do a whole kitchen full of props—toast up in the air, or pancakes; you know, the stuff we've done over the years. Vivian could never do it. She just died every time she had to touch a prop.

But Buster taught me the value of props and the value of taking care of them, checking them yourself, even how to make some of them, but especially how to make them work. I haven't had a great many fights with directors, but I had a real battle with my first director on television. I guess it's because I was frightened. I had to handle the first pop-up toaster we used, and during the rehearsals they gave me pieces of balsa wood that were taking off like ping-pong balls. I said, "Don't you think we ought to start working with bread?" He got a little miffed. So I said, "Well, it's my bread, bring it in." What a hell of a difference! The balsa went here, and the bread went there. The more you work with props the better.

Since 1960 you've made only five feature films. Why haven't you done more?

BALL: Well, when I was in pictures before television, I didn't dig it too much, because I wasn't typecast. You have to start someplace. I started as a model because I looked like a model, and as "the other woman" or "the career girl" because I have a deep, aggressive voice that has no softness or romance to it. Fifteen years in pictures and I'd always been playing someone else. I wasn't a recognizable personality like Cary Grant or Gary Cooper or Gable.

Then when television came along, I said, "Gee, this is my chance to be typed," which is the opposite of what most people want to do. I said, "I want to be . . . what *do* I want to be?" I had to stop and think. And I thought, "Well, of the thirty or so pictures I've made, what did I like best?" I could find only three or four scenes in those pictures that I cared anything about, and they were domestic scenes, where I was a housewife—normal, natural, somewhat silly—but I loved the domestic scenes. So I started from that.

The other reason I didn't want to make pictures is that I had made them for so long and I didn't like the hours. I was married to a man [Desi Arnaz] who was on the road [as a bandleader], and you can't have a baby long-distance. We wanted to stay home. So I said, "Maybe television is good for a year or two." In the meantime, pictures changed and you always had to go on location. Very few pictures were being made here after the demise of Papa Mayer and Cohn [Louis B. Mayer and Harry Cohn, heads of MGM and Columbia]. There were no more papas, there were no more studios, there were no more umbrellas. I missed that, because I'm a family person. I like to be protected, I like to be told what to do, believe it or not. And then came the nudies, and I didn't fit them.

All those years you maintained that basic Lucy character—a kind of Everywoman, a very basic American person. Was there a model for that in your mind? How much of that was you, and how did you maintain the character as your own life got farther away from that?

BALL: My own life never got far away from that, because that's all I've ever played, except for a little difference in the very beginning, a dependency upon Ricky [her husband, played by Arnaz]. In the beginning I was always trying to outmaneuver him and get into show biz. But the basic woman has become less childish, I think. It's just a matter of growing up. When you're playing the mother of your own kids, or any kids, you don't act quite as childish as you do when you're outmaneuvering your new husband. I'm glad to hear you say that you think the woman has remained basically the same, but I think she has matured through the scripts.

You have stressed repeatedly that your character is an American character, and yet—

BALL: She's international.

I was about to say so. Your series have had tremendous success abroad.

BALL: The marvelous thing about the Lucy show is that there has been so much physical comedy. That's great for the foreign countries. We play in seventy-seven countries. The physical stuff is not very difficult for them to understand. They don't have to follow the words.

Could you tell us about your vaudeville act?

BALL: CBS said, "We want you to go into television, but we think that your husband—well, no one would believe that he is your husband." I said, "Why not? We're married." "Well, he's Cuban and you're playing an American family." I said, "Let's go out and test it." That's why we went out. I didn't play very long. I got pregnant.

You've been in television for twenty years, and the basic character has changed on each show because her relationships to the different supporting characters have changed.

BALL: You're absolutely right, but it's just circumstances. Bill Frawley [the Fred character] died, and that broke up that cast. And Desi and I got a divorce, and that certainly broke it up. But Vivian and I tried it because CBS wanted us to; we were very successful. Then Vivian got very ill, and she also got married and moved away, and she didn't want to commute. I understood it. I cried a lot. But it just wasn't the same.

The first setup in *I Love Lucy* was a fine marriage of writers, two generations of people, no kids, then the kids came along, and the kids grew up. And every time I sold the film to syndication I had to change the format. I could remain Lucy, but I had to change the people around me. My kids were at an age when they weren't doing too well in school; they were not working up to their potential. I said to Gary [Morton, her second husband and producer], "Can't we take them out of school? Let's change the format of the show—maybe the kids would like to be in it again." A wonderful thing happened: they found their way, they found a direction, Lucie in particular. Desi has never been right for comedy, but he's doing very well in the dramatic stuff.

You're one of the very few women in this business who has endured with a certain amount of independence and power over the years, as an actress and then as an executive. I wonder if you could pin down the problems of being a woman in those cases.

BALL: I haven't found any.

How did you get into the business end?

BALL: The business end I inherited after many years quite by accident [through her divorce from Arnaz]. I liked having my small company. I didn't like running three studios at all. I was only running a studio to sell it. I inherited a lot of buildings, but I did not dig running big business. I liked having my comedy-acting workshop, I liked helping young kids, and I did my job, but it almost put me away. I had to oversee all the productions and make all the big decisions, but with the help of a very trusted board of trustees, the bank, the lawyers, the producers, and the directors. I had a lot of people I had to trust implicitly, or I wouldn't have done any of this. I came back to a studio that was a raging steamboat and it was sinking, and I had to build it up to get a setup. At one time we had fifteen or sixteen shows. But I don't like to hire and fire, and I don't feel capable of making those big decisions. That's why I got out of it.

A lot of actors and actresses switch over after a time and become directors. Have you thought about that?

BALL: Only on my own show. I've had to do it many times, because we've been training people. I don't feel I'd want to do anybody else's show. I could perhaps direct my daughter's show. But I don't feel like becoming a director. I like my own little niche. I'm so damned glad when I find a director who knows what he's doing. But I've never had any great directors—one great I had, Vincente Minnelli [on *Ziegfeld Follies*]. I've never had any great parts, for that matter.

What do you think makes a good director?

BALL: Right or wrong, you must have a point of view. Good or bad, you've got to know what you want. It's authority. Also, in working with an actor, it's that authority—not hitting him over the head with it, but your point of view coming through. It has to be like that.

And you have to do your homework. *Boy,* you have to do your homework. You have to have a knowledge of how to do it, then you have to have people around you who know how to do it, and you have to know whether or not they know their job. I prided myself on recognizing a good photographer, a good still photographer, a good prop man, a good special-effects man. Any director gets a group around him, and any great gaffer [head electrician] has his first man, and they know how to keep them throughout the years. But it's a group thing. You build your own stock company, get your little group together that you can depend on. It's a matter of authority and knowledge, vitality, and keeping your health.

Comedy relies so much on timing, and film or tape imposes a different kind of timing. How closely do you work with your direc-

*tors on TV so you don't do a bit that is very funny live and then
lose it on film or tape?*

BALL: We do our cutting as we work. The only time we're in
trouble is when we have a great spread [time overrun], a big audience which applauds too long or laughs a little longer than we
expected. We go in knowing where our laughs are supposed to be,
and about how long they will be. We've learned that Gale Gordon
cannot even walk onstage without there being applause, he cannot
take a deep breath without getting a laugh. That took a few years
to learn.

Do you work with directors you know very well?

BALL: I've worked with the same people for many, many years.
Also technical people and writers. We brought in camera coordi-
nators; we pioneered that [*I Love Lucy* was the first three-camera
TV show]. We made up that job, and that gentleman [Karl
Freund] trained several others, and we brought assistant directors
in and made them directors, and took second assistants and made
them first assistants and unit managers and moved them up.

There's one thing I pride myself on—knowing how to do my
show. I don't know how to do your show, or his show, or their
show. I know about my show. So I got the title of ogre: "Oh,
Jesus, don't work with her, growl, growl." I had a couple of bad
directors who didn't know what they were doing. They were nice
guys, they didn't give me too much trouble, but I'd say, "Listen,
you've got to bring him up, he's got a funny part and he's not pro-
jecting." And they'd go and do it. Maybe they didn't see it. You've
got to see it awful fast to beat me on my show.

*One of the pieces we just saw was the one with Wally Cox when
you take over for him and lead the orchestra, which is one of the
funniest pieces of comedy I've ever seen. Do you set up each bit?*

BALL: Right. I had a great director—I still have him, Jack Dono-
hue. He knew what to do with that. That was a particularly wonderful script, it was there in black and white, but it was a task and
it really frightened me. Those were all real musicians in there,
too, and we had only three hours—an hour here, an hour there.
My writers had it down. Madelyn wrote, "She looks here, she
thinks about that, then she figures, 'Well, take a look at the sheet,'
takes her time, wiggles around, she has plenty of time to dawdle—
oh, suddenly, it's time to ring that silly thing." That was all there.

And you know what our greatest trouble was on that? To stop the symphony boys from laughing. They ruined takes because they hadn't seen enough rehearsal.

So none of that was ad-libbed?

BALL: There's very little ad-libbing on my show. I have to have an economy of words because of the timing. I have to allow for a minute, minute-and-a-half spread—if I get more than that I'm in trouble. Everyone scatters like the four winds after Thursday night. The people we hire for that particular show are not there next week. If it were just a family we could retake something, which we very seldom do.

We work in front of an audience, always have. It's very important to me to have an audience there because they're a cross-section of America—which is marvelous, because there's a great difference in the people of America from one side to the other, what they laugh at, what they like, what they think, what they understand. The writing is done three or four months ahead, we read it three or four times, it goes back and forth from first draft into second draft, third draft—finally comes Monday at ten A.M. and the new actors are all there, the cast is there, they're seeing it for the first time, and Thursday afternoon we put it on for three or four hundred people.

How did you get started in show business?

BALL: I always wanted to be in vaudeville. I didn't know it was dead. When I arrived in New York City I was going to get into vaudeville because that's all I had ever seen. I had seen some pictures, but it never dawned on me to be in pictures. I had gotten into everything I could in high school and church and Sunday school and the Elks convention or whatever came along in my hometown [Jamestown, New York]. I was in there pitching, dancing, and singing. So I kept looking for vaudeville, and I didn't even know the Palace was closed. I never got a job—never got near anybody—and finally I got so hungry I went into modeling.

The great thing was that I kept my eye on show biz. I wasn't just going to run off and marry the first guy who asked me. I thought, I have to learn how to do something, so I'll learn how to be a good model. I couldn't dance, I wasn't beautiful, nobody was yelling for anything I had.

So, I was walking down the street one day—this is a true story

—a very hot July day, and a lady who had seen me in a fashion show said, "What are you doing here in July? Nobody stays in town in July." I said, "I'm working." She had just come from the Sam Goldwyn office, and she said there was an opening for a show-girl for six weeks in an Eddie Cantor picture, *Roman Scandals*. I said, "Anything to get out of town for six weeks." In ten minutes I had a job. They had no choice. They were desperate. If I'd been tested I probably never would have gotten it, because I wasn't beautiful, *zaftig*, or any of the things these girls were.

The picture, instead of taking six weeks, took six months. After six months I felt a part of something and I thought I could learn. I went over and joined a stock company at Columbia, and I learned a little by having a lot of seltzer water squirted in my face by the Three Stooges. Nice men, *but* . . . . I learned a lot of things about comedy that I never want to do. I just worked on and on.

I had showgirl friends who complained: "Why would you do a thing like that?" It used to bother them that I'd get into black-face and scream. I did it because nobody else would do it. Eddie Cantor remembered it, so I got three or four other things from Mr. Cantor. I was glad because I learned from Mr. Cantor, and he was pleased because I learned and I didn't complain. I never really complained. I loved the business that much.

I feel sorry for you people. You don't have the chance to hang around like I did as a showgirl, a script girl, a contract player. You don't have the studios now. That's why a lot of kids are prostitut-ing themselves in pornos these days—to make a living. They think that's the only way to do it. Well, *you* know that's not true. That's why you're here.

James Wong Howe

James Wong Howe was one of the masters of black-and-white photography in motion pictures. Also honored for his late experiments in color, Howe photographed 125 films in a career that began in 1917 and lasted until 1975. A native of China, he was among the first minority-group members to achieve great success in Hollywood.

Howe was nominated for ten Academy Awards and won two, for *The Rose Tattoo* and *Hud*. Dubbed "Low-Key Howe" in the early 1930s because of his penchant for dark, moody lighting, he developed a supple style that combined dramatic realism with elegance of composition and a sensitivity to the finest nuances of light. His many notable films include the silent *Peter Pan* as well as *The Power and the Glory*; *The Thin Man*; *Algiers*; *Kings Row*; *Yankee Doodle Dandy*; *Air Force*; *Objective Burma!*; *Body and Soul*; *Come Back, Little Sheba*; *Picnic*; *Seconds*; and *The Molly Maguires*, perhaps his finest achievement in color.

Born Wong Tung Jim in Kwantung, China, in 1899, Howe came to the United States in 1904. His father was a railroad laborer who later became a storekeeper and ranch owner in Oregon. The son began using a still camera at the age of twelve, but after his father died he drifted through a series of odd jobs, including farm laboring and boxing.

After working as a dark-room assistant in a Los Angeles photographic studio, he was hired as a janitor in the camera room of Lasky Studios in 1917 and two years later became an assistant to Cecil B. DeMille's cameraman, Alvin Wykoff. Silent star Mary Miles Minter promoted him to full cameraman in 1922 after being impressed with his still photography.

Howe experienced some prejudice as an Oriental in Hollywood, but his novelty also worked to his advantage and, combined with his engaging personality, made him the most-publicized of all Hollywood cameramen. Directors regarded him highly because of his intense dedication to all aspects of filmmaking, although in his later years he acquired the reputation of being autocratic. Howe himself directed several films and television shows, including *Go, Man Go!*, a 1954 feature with the Harlem Globetrotters, and *The World of Dong Kingman*, a short about the noted Chinese painter.

Health problems forced Howe into retirement after *The Molly Maguires* in 1969, but in 1975 he was summoned back to replace Vilmos Zsigmond on *Funny Lady*. He died on July 12, 1976.

SELECTED FILMOGRAPHY

1922 *Drums of Fate*   1923 *The Trail of the Lonesome Pine* 1924 *Peter Pan*   1927 *The Rough Riders*   1931 *Transatlantic* / *The Criminal Code* / *The Yellow Ticket*   1932 *Chandu the Magician*   1933 *Hello, Sister (Walking Down Broadway)* / *The Power and the Glory* / *Viva Villa!*   1934 *The Thin Man* / *Manhattan Melodrama*   1935 *Mark of the Vampire*   1936 *Fire Over England*   1937 *The Prisoner of Zenda* / *The Adventures of Tom Sawyer*   1938 *Algiers*   1939 *They Made Me a Criminal* / *Abe Lincoln in Illinois*   1940 *The Story of Dr. Ehrlich's Magic Bullet* / *City for Conquest* / *The Strawberry Blonde*   1941 *Kings Row*   1942 *Yankee Doodle Dandy* / *Hangmen Also Die*   1943 *Air Force*   1945 *Objective Burma!*   1947 *Pursued* / *Body and Soul*   1948 *Mr. Blandings Builds His Dream House*   1950 *The*

Baron of Arizona   1951 *The Brave Bulls | He Ran All the Way*
1953 *Come Back, Little Sheba*   1955 *The Rose Tattoo | Picnic*
1957 *The Sweet Smell of Success | The Old Man and the Sea*
1957 *Bell, Book, and Candle*   1959 *The Last Angry Man*   1962
Hud   1966 *Seconds | This Property Is Condemned*   1968 *The
Heart Is a Lonely Hunter*   1969 *The Molly Maguires*   1975
Funny Lady

THE SEMINAR

James Wong Howe held seminars with the Fellows of the Center for Advanced Film Studies, in conjunction with the American Society of Cinematographers, on April 7 and 14, 1973.

You said once that the photography should always convey the story rather than just stimulate the viewer. I wonder if at any point you found yourself in conflict with the director about this?
HOWE: In the relationship between the camera and the director, the most difficult thing to find is a director who will cooperate with the cameraman and vice versa. The director, of course, thinks of his action with his actor, and we think mostly in terms of lighting. Whenever you move the camera, you're going to complicate the lighting. You're going to have more work to do, because in order to balance when someone walks from one end of the room to the other, you've got to light it so there's a certain smoothness. An actor can walk through dark spaces; I think that's good, because it gives a little more movement. But if you're photographing a motion picture, you've got a story to tell, and you can't always keep your actors in the dark. You've got to read their expressions. That's why they have close-ups.

Now, with many of the old-time directors, like Howard Hawks and John Ford, you always find that their films are beautifully photographed and there is not a lot of movement. I feel that camera movement must have a purpose. I don't say that we do away with camera movement, but it must be done in a way that helps to tell the story. Ford never moves a camera unless he has to move. He moves a camera to follow the actors. In making the film, we are all subservient to the story. The story is the thing. So, how can we keep you believing that this is a real thing going on?
How do you go about determining the light balance?
HOWE: It depends on what your subject is. If you're making a murder mystery, naturally there are shadows. I don't know why there'd be more shadows in a murder mystery, because murders are committed in all different places, but every time you see one on TV, you've got shadows that travel from the ground to the ceiling. That's the handiwork of the cameraman and also the director. Does it need doing? I don't know.

Try to be honest. Try to find a simple way of doing things. In 1927 I worked on a film called *Underworld*, directed by Josef von Sternberg. I thought, at that stage of my career, that I knew everything—"God, nothing to it. All you do is throw a few lights in there." So I had a shot with three nuns walking past a cement wall outdoors. I took some brutes [large lights] and hit the nuns, and I thought, "That's good. Now I need another one from here. Now I need another one from *here*." Mind you, this is supposed to be sunlight. When the three nuns walked past the wall I had nine shadows. Von Sternberg said, "Jimmy, one sun cannot throw nine shadows." Well, I thought, if I kill all these lights I won't get an exposure. This is where I admire directors who have the courage, the knowledge, the authority to back up the cameraman. He said, "Look, Jimmy, kill those lights and shoot it with that one. Now we see three nuns and we see three shadows. That look more like sunlight?" We shot it. It looked beautiful. I learned something. Today I never get more than one shadow at one time.

Now, if I were photographing the group in here [the AFI seminar room], my main source of light is coming through that window. We call that the key. This side here [opposite to the side facing the window] is always the shadow side. We have a huge room—I would like to take maybe one or two soft lights up there. That would act as my fill light [light to augment the natural sunlight]. And that's all I would need. If I had to duplicate this kind of setting in the studio, I would play a strong light through the window, with a fill light in the foreground here, and always keep that same angle. Don't hit one face this way and the other one that way. Same way if you're going to light a moonlight shot: one light. Now, you can't cover the whole area with one light, so you may have to use three. You establish the angle right for the first lamp and you blend the other one in the same angle. Don't shoot it so that when a person walks the shadow jumps from one place to the other.

Do you like to use a light meter?

HOWE: When I started, we didn't have schools for photography. We just had to learn it by mistake, error. We didn't have light meters. We had to judge the exposure by looking through the camera, either through the ground glass [the lens] or sometimes through a piece of film. It's very easy, you know, to take a light meter; you can buy any kind, and you get proper exposure. But there's one thing that meter will not tell you—whether you've got the right mood or not. That you'll have to decide for yourself. When I'm lighting, naturally I measure my key light sometimes. Now I can look at it and get a good idea of what it is, which comes from experience and practice. You begin to get a feel of light. When you start filling, you don't need a meter, because if you do it with a meter, you do it by numbers and you won't get the kind of mood that you feel yourself. You've got to look at that scene, and the nature of the scene itself will invariably dictate to you what kind of mood you want to give it. That's when you begin to really use light.

I must tell you a very funny story. Years ago, I opened a Chinese restaurant out in the San Fernando Valley. They wanted a picture of me in front of the restaurant to run in the paper. So one day a photographer appeared. It was on Ventura Boulevard, and traffic was really heavy; he got out there and set up an eight-by-ten [a still camera on a tripod]. He's under a black cloth with his rear end sticking out and he's trying to get a focus with cars honking at him, and I thought, "Oh, gee, this guy is going to get hit." So I said, "Look, put your wide-angle lens on and come in here on the sidewalk and you'll get the whole thing." He said, "You take care of your damn noodles, I'll take care of this." Then he said, "I want a close-up. Stand in front of that door there." I said OK. He stuck the meter up in front of my nose. I said, "I'd just stop it down to 11—give it a tenth of a second." He said, "You're a hell of a good guesser, aren't you?"

So, you see, you can learn exposure if you observe light, because in photography the most important thing is light. Study light. That's what gives you the mood, not so much the composition. It's the light—sunny light, the quality of light, the texture of light—you can almost feel it. See, there's light all around this room. You can't see it unless it strikes something, but it didn't blow a puff of smoke. You see the light because it hit the smoke. Learn to see. Learn to feel light—at night, walking the street, or whenever you're driving, any time of day, afternoon, evening. Some places have a long twilight. It's a beautiful quality of light, especially for color. You don't need only sunlight for color. You can get wonderful effects on overcast days, foggy days—go up to San Francisco sometime when the fog comes rolling in.

One time I drove across the Golden Gate Bridge, had my little 16-millimeter camera; I always carry it around, because I use it like a notebook. And there was this wonderful shot: I could see the structure of the bridge sticking out and down below it was all fog. So I'm sitting there in front, photographing, and suddenly we come into the fog and it just grays out, and then we see a car coming with the headlights, like ghosts with two yellow beaming lights, and I just hung onto it—I wanted to see what happened. Suddenly it opened up and the sun struck San Francisco and it was beautiful! It was just like somebody opened a curtain, very theatrical.

How do you feel about the use of soft light?

HOWE: I don't care what kind of light you use as long as you can control it and make it do what you want it to. Ask yourself why you want to do it. You must have a specific reason before you think you want to use soft light. You don't want to use it just because it's soft, because the shadow is soft. Maybe if you have a soft candle in the scene, or if you want to duplicate a north light, I think it's wonderful, but I wouldn't go overboard with all the soft-light things.

Same with a lens. Say you've got a man walking into a huge cathedral from the back and you use a wide-angle lens. The reason? Because you want to get in the ceiling and the altar. Now you want to get a close-up of him looking up there. So what do you do now? You put on a three-inch lens. You shoot his close-up. What happens to the cathedral? It disappears in back of him. You're not in the cathedral anymore. You lost it by using the three-inch lens. When you reverse what you're looking at you should use the same lens you shot with when you came in, because from the back you always want to see that perspective also. It's the same rule.

What's your favorite hard lens?

HOWE: My favorite is the 30-millimeter. First of all, it gives me the right feeling of perspective. It's a little forced. They say the 50-millimeter is closest to our vision, but I like the 30, because it gives me just a little more than our vision. The 50 is just right down to what we see in focus, but we see a little more off the side with a 30 than with a 50. And another thing, without having stopped down [increased the light exposure] too far, I can carry the depth of field a little more, because today I like to see a little more sharpness.

You must remember that pictures are a commercial business. There are many theaters. If you happen to get into a good first-run house you get good projection, but you shouldn't neglect the fellow who has to see it in a second run in a little house. In recent years I haven't used diffusion very much, because by the time they project through the dirty glass, the projectionist has already put a diffusion glass in front of the lens.

Which do you prefer, black and white or color?

HOWE: I personally like black and white. To me it's much more of a challenge than color. Color separates itself. In early-day pictures they used so much backlight to keep the images from blending into the background that you didn't know where all that backlight was coming from: you'd go into a boxcar and suddenly you'd see a lot of backlight and the door was closed.

The last picture I made was *The Molly Maguires,* an old nineteenth-century mining story set in Pennsylvania, an expensive film. The director, Martin Ritt, whom I respect very much, did a beautiful job on it. He said, "Look, fellows, I wanted to make this picture very much, so we're going to have to make it in color, but I want you to make a color picture look like black and white." Somebody had told him about desaturation [muting color in the laboratory]. I think it's a trick. I don't think it accomplishes very much. The lab men—most of them—are not really artists, they're technicians, and you can't expect them to get the kind of emotional feeling out of color that you like to have yourself. And once they do it, you're stuck with it.

So I said, "I don't want to fool around with it. If you're going to try to keep the color down, you've got to do it from the very beginning. The costume designer has to get the material and we've got to make some tests, and the art director has to keep the bright paint off the houses."

The houses were all different colors, and they had to put false woodwork over them and paint it a dark, dirty gray-green. When we first saw the trees, they were just branches. They were wonderful against this gray sky, these dark branches sticking up, and the director said, "Oh, Jimmy, we've got to keep that effect." But when we went back to Pennsylvania, it was in the spring and the buds had started coming out. "So what are we going to do, Jimmy?" I said, "Better hire some natives and have them pick the buds off." So we had dozens of guys with ladders, picking the buds off. They thought we were crazy.

We shot the foreground, but in the background, each time we saw more leaves, more leaves. We lost the whole feeling, because the atmosphere in the background has so much to do with the foreground. The background became a beautiful, soft, spring green. It was too pretty. So we got a helicopter and blew black dust all over the whole countryside.

In the course of your career did you often have to do films you didn't want to do?

HOWE: Yes. You know, when you're under contract to the studios you don't have many choices. You're assigned, because they don't let you lie around very much. I remember when I signed my first contract in 1922, they said, "Jimmy, whether you work or not, you get paid." I found I worked every week except two weeks a year. They never let me lie around. If I wasn't shooting a film, I had to go shoot second unit, I had to shoot inserts, but that was wonderful—I learned a lot. I could afford to make mistakes because it didn't cost much to make them over.

Film is a wonderful expression. All of us must learn the technique very well, just like a sculptor with a piece of raw clay. You can mold it the way you want it, and a cameraman can take lights, camera, film, lenses, and do anything you want with it. I think today films are becoming much more an art form, and you don't really have to go into a motion-picture studio to make feature films. There are so many things you can do—documentary, teaching things, science films. On TV, the things that Jacques Cousteau does underwater, these are wonderful things to do. Exciting. Adventure. Maybe not all the glamour that you would have with movie stars, but after you see two or three movie stars, they're all the same.

How does a cameraman handle the stars?

HOWE: You have to be very nice to the stars. I want you all to understand that you have to deal with personalities, especially stars, and they can make you as a cameraman or break you as a cameraman. If they like your work, they insist on your being their cameraman. For many years, William Daniels was Greta Garbo's cameraman. She wouldn't do a film without him. So that gives you a great security. When you go to work in the studio, you should know your technique very well, because you're going to find out that you're not dealing as much with technique as you are with people. You've got the producer to please. And you've got to please your laboratory. And the director. And the art director. You've got so many people to please that you wonder "When am I going to please myself?"

I was doing a picture at MGM called *The Thin Man* with William Powell, the very first one. The art director complained that I wasn't lighting up the sets enough. I didn't want to light too much because I wanted to keep the background dark: I felt to suggest something was much more exciting than to actually see it. Sometimes it's not how much light you use to get an effect, but how little you use and still make it work. I had a star one time who could only be photographed on one side—I don't know whether left or right—but the art director built the door for the wrong side. You know what? They changed the door. When he came in it swung one way, when he went out it swung the other way. Nobody knew the difference, but he was happy.

How do you feel about the director of photography being a separate job from the camera operator?

HOWE: Today there's so much going on for the director of photography. He has to concentrate on his lighting; it would be difficult for him to operate the camera too. But at the same time it depends on the operator you have. If you have one who really knows your requirements and understands composition, he can be very helpful. On the other hand, if he doesn't understand composition and he doesn't know how to crop, it can be devastating. On some shots, if you feel you have a certain movement or composition you want to finish on, the union will allow a cameraman to make one special shot like that. But one shouldn't make a habit of doing it, because, in the first place, it embarrasses the operator. In the second place, you do a man out of a job.

See, there's a reason for a union. I've worked in the industry since 1917 and we didn't have a union then. I remember going to work at seven in the morning and working until around seven the next morning; they'd send you home and they'd call you back at ten that same morning. I remember working at Fox twenty-six hours without stopping. They'd give you a sandwich. You'd be working eating a sandwich. You never got overtime. In the early days we used to have to hand-crank our camera. We didn't have motors, so when you wanted to learn to be a cameraman, the first thing you did as an assistant was to grind that camera as much as you could—just keep turning it, to get rhythm. I couldn't take a camera home to my room, so I bought a little coffee grinder, and I used to sit and crank that. And that's how I learned to crank the rhythm.

Do you always try to work with the same unit?

HOWE: It's kind of a family group when you have a unit. The cameraman has his own operator and assistants—the gaffer [the head electrican], his grip, and his stand-by painter [to paint sets for mood and color effect]. Usually when you're under contract you keep that unit together. But today these groups are often broken up. It was a wonderful relationship in the early days, because that gave an opportunity for the assistant and the operator to study the cameraman's style and his method of working. If the assistant saw something, he could come up to me and say, "Jimmy, why do you do that?" I took time to explain it to him, because I remembered that when I had to learn I asked the same thing.

Once I asked a cameraman and he said, "Do you think I'm going to tell you in ten minutes what it took me ten years to learn?" I felt very, very embarrassed, and I said, "If I ever become a cameraman, I hope I'll never say that, because everybody wants to learn." I taught at UCLA one semester in 1965 and I learned a great deal from the students. The kind of questions they were asking never came up to me before; I had to answer them, and by exchanging opinions I learned a great deal. So we all learn from each other.

How do you visualize a shot? Do you do it by looking through the camera or do you do it more in your mind?

HOWE: When I look at a thing, I have a frame of reference, after years of looking through the lens. One thing I would say: if you have a horizon line, never let it come in the middle of the screen. If you have a cloudy sky and a sailboat, don't split the water and the sky in half, because that doesn't give you composition. You have to make up your mind. You've got to say either the water is more interesting or the sky is. Now, if I had a daytime shot, with the sailboat sailing and the sky was beautiful with clouds, and I wanted an open-air feeling, I would use more sky than water. If I had a sunset shot, I probably would give more water, because I would see that reflection come right up to the lens, since the sun is below the horizon; so I would put the horizon line up above the center.

The same way when you're shooting extreme close-ups. The eyes and the mouth are the most important thing when you get right up close. They convey the thought. The top of the head does not have to be in. It's just wasted space. Concentrate on what you want to tell the audience. Make them look at the eyes.

Do you have any favorite shots?

HOWE: I always have one shot or maybe two in a picture that I particularly like, and sometimes they're cut out and thrown on the floor. I had one in *The Molly Maguires* where Richard Harris was writing a letter home, and I just lit it with a little peanut bulb. I loved the shot, but they threw it out on me. I had one shot in *Hud* where Paul Newman and his nephew, Brandon DeWilde, had just come back from drinking beer. They had been in a fight, they're dousing themselves with water, and they walk toward the back of the house, the porch. I had it lit with the light all coming from the porch and splatting on the ground. I liked that shot. It was a very simple shot.

What were the shots that gave you the biggest problems?

HOWE: There are always problems, because the writers use their imagination and then the cameraman has to figure out how to photograph it. Directors sometimes pick impossible angles. But there are very few problems that cannot be solved. I don't know of any in pictures. They say, "You can't do this" or "You can't do that," but I think there are a lot of rules that are made to be broken in photography. To be a photographer, you've got to have a lot of courage. You've got to stick your neck out. You're liable to get some scars, but it's worth trying.

I'll give you a little example. I was on a film called *Air Force* at Warner Brothers during World War II. Howard Hawks was the director, a fine director and a wonderful man. He had a shot where nine B-17s were coming in to land. They were supposed to be in Pearl Harbor, but we were making it in Florida. It was just after sunset, so I had to line up all my lights and get the generator. About two, three hours before we had to make a shot, I asked the electrician to light all the lights to try it out, and he said, "Jimmy, we're having problems. The generator doesn't work." I told Howard. He said, "That's not my problem; that's your problem." So I went to the special-effects man and said, "Look, do we have any three-minute flares?" He said, "I got a flock of them." What I did was to take the reflectors off the back of the lights and hang them on stands. Then I stuck these flares in front of the reflectors and had the electrician wire them up. We tried a couple and it worked.

So here come these planes (if I ever prayed to Buddha, I'd really . . .) , and I told him to hit the switch. All these flares came on and they flickered, and it was wonderful because the landing field was supposed to be on fire. The smoke from the flares drifted across, and these planes coming down with the landing lamps going through the smoke and the propellers swirling this smoke, it created a lot of drama. Hawks knew how it looked without even seeing the rushes. He said, "Gee, that's great, Jimmy, wonderful effect. Send the generator home—we're shooting all this with the flares." If the generator hadn't broken, I wouldn't have gotten this effect.

Another time, I was in New York directing a film called *Go, Man, Go!*, about the Harlem Globetrotters. Elia Kazan had just finished *On the Waterfront*. He heard I was in town and he called me. He said, "Jimmy, I have some shots I need to make and I have problems." So we went down to the docks to do some shots for the ending. It was an overcast day. The production manager said, "How many lights do you want?" I said, "No lights." "*No lights?*" We shot, and it got later and later and darker and darker. Finally I said, "Gee, Gadge [Kazan's nickname], this is about it." He said, "I've got one close-up to do." We had a couple of station wagons there to hold the equipment. I said, "Bring them over and put them on high beam," and we just shone the headlights on Karl Malden and shot it. It worked. In color, it may've gone a little red, but since it was late afternoon, you could justify it.

Then Kazan said, "Now I need a shot of Brando. He's been beaten up, so he's dizzy and he's walking into the warehouse as the door opens." We shot that with his feet staggering and a close-up of him: we had a hand-held camera, an Eyemo [a small camera originally developed for newsreel photography], and I gave it to the operator. I put a chalk mark on the cement and said, "Now, look through that camera and walk around that chalk mark." He said, "Gee, I'm getting a little dizzy." I spun him around and said, "Keep walking. Keep walking." He said, "I'm dizzy." I said, "OK, now point the camera at that door, hit the trigger, and walk." It photographed, you see? He couldn't walk very steady, so it made a wonderful shot to reflect how Brando was seeing.

These are the things that are a great deal of fun in making films. You can use your imagination and intuition, your reflexes. It's frustrating at times. This is a business in which you get ulcers. But I always believed why should *I* get ulcers? Give *them* ulcers.

Leonard Rosenman

One of the most sophisticated musical composers in motion-picture history, Leonard Rosenman has been profoundly influential in helping to bring film music into the mainstream of modern composition. In his dual career as a composer of concert music and film scores, he has successfully blended both disciplines into a mutually enriching whole.

Rosenman has won two Academy Awards, both for adaptation scores: Stanley Kubrick's eighteenth-century Thackeray panorama, *Barry Lyndon* (1975), and Hal Ashby's elegaic rendering of the life of folksinger Woody Guthrie, *Bound for Glory* (1976). But he is best known for his early film work on two James Dean classics, Elia Kazan's *East of Eden* and Nicholas Ray's *Rebel Without a Cause*, both released in 1955. Rosenman's mixture of romanticism with an innovative use of jarring modern tonalities was a major reason for those films' imprint on the popular consciousness.

Born in New York in 1924, Rosenman first concentrated on painting, but after returning from service in the Air Force in World War II he turned to music. He studied theory and composition under Arnold Schoenberg, who developed the twelve-tone

111

system that greatly influenced Rosenman's subsequent film work.

Through the years Rosenman has written many choral and chamber pieces as well as an opera, and he has conducted orchestras and chamber groups across the United States and overseas. He has also been a professor of music at the University of Southern California, California Institute of the Arts, and the University of Illinois, and has lectured at UC Berkeley.

Rosenman turned to films after James Dean, one of his piano pupils in New York, took director Elia Kazan to a concert of Rosenman's at the Museum of Modern Art. Kazan hired Rosenman to score *East of Eden*, for which the composer was given unusual creative latitude. His subsequent film work has covered a wide range of material, from war movies to fantasies to Westerns to horror films; among them are *The Young Stranger, The Savage Eye, The Rise and Fall of Legs Diamond, Hell Is for Heroes, Fantastic Voyage, A Man Called Horse, Cross Creek,* and James Bridges's 1977 film *9/30/55*, which interweaves Rosenman's scores for the two Dean films with a story taking place on the day of the star's death.

For television Rosenman has scored such series as *The Defenders, Combat, The Virginian, Kojak,* and *Marcus Welby*; Jane Goodall's wildlife documentaries; and the TV movies *Sybil* and *Friendly Fire,* for which he won Emmy Awards.

In the last few years he has returned increasingly to concert music, and retrospective performances of his concert compositions have been held in Los Angeles and New York.

FILMOGRAPHY

1955 *East of Eden / The Cobweb / Rebel Without a Cause*
1956 *Edge of the City* 1957 *The Young Stranger / Bombers B-52* 1958 *Lafayette Escadrille / The Hidden World* 1959 *Pork Chop Hill* 1960 *The Savage Eye / The Rise and Fall of Legs Diamond / The Bramble Bush / The Crowded Sky / The Plunderers* 1961 *The Outsider / Hell Is for Heroes* 1962 *Convicts 4 / The Chapman Report* 1966 *Fantastic Voyage* 1967 *A Covenant with Death* 1968 *Countdown / Hellfighters* 1970 *A Man Called Horse / Beneath the Planet of the Apes* 1971

Skipper / *The Todd Killings* 1973 *Battle for the Planet of the Apes* 1975 *Race with the Devil* / *Barry Lyndon* 1976 *Birch Interval* / *Bound for Glory* 1977 *The Car* / *Sybil* (TV) / *9/30/55* 1978 *An Enemy of the People* / *Lord of the Rings* 1979 *Friendly Fire* (TV) / *Promises in the Dark* / *Prophecy* 1980 *Hide in Plain Sight* / *The Jazz Singer* 1982 *Making Love* 1983 *Cross Creek*

THE SEMINAR

Leonard Rosenman held seminars with the Fellows of the Center for Advanced Film Studies on January 28, 1975, and February 14, 1979.

Are some films better off without music?
ROSENMAN: Yes, a lot of them are. There's too much music in movies. When I first started to work in films I worked at Warner Brothers, and they had wall-to-wall music. If the film was an hour and a half long the score was an hour and a half long. At that time the last of the filmic Mesozoic giants, Jack Warner, was the head of the studio; he had been indoctrinated very strongly by his own experience in silent films. The function of music in the silent films was to add sound effects and also to cover up all kinds of realistic sounds—popcorn, the toilet flushing, the projection machine—to remove the idea of reality so that the audience would be able to suspend disbelief. The minute you suspend disbelief you are in films. Like most of the early pioneers in films, Jack evidently felt that music had a magical mystery power, a subliminal power. So they began to use it indiscriminately. It was like an enema in the Jewish family tradition. "It can't hurt you" was the idea.

They did not realize that diminishing returns set in—that if you had music from frame alpha to frame omega, you had come back to the original idea of the silents: after a while you didn't hear the music anymore. If you happen to see an old Warner Brothers movie like *Anthony Adverse* [1937], those films with wall-to-wall music, after a while you feel like saying, "Stop the music!" Music couldn't possibly do for the audience what Jack and the other old filmmakers felt music could do. Because if you don't hear it, why use it? Max Steiner, who did the music for *Anthony Adverse*, was a creator of a kind of Mickey Mouse music [a term describing music that mimics the action on screen], so that if a man in a film walked along with a club foot, the music walked along with him with a club foot. Max is very important in our craft, of course, because he wrote the first original score to a film, which was *King Kong*. He made an outstanding contribution to movies.

You changed the types of music used in films with your introduction in 1955 of serial and twelve-tone scoring [serial music is modern composition that discards traditional rules and conventions; the twelve-tone system, devised by Arnold Schoenberg in the 1920s, involves systematic use of all twelve tones of the chromatic scale]. What kinds of problems did you have with these innovations?

ROSENMAN: Alex North and I are credited with bringing film music into the twentieth century. When I came on the scene in 1954 to do *East of Eden*, I was an ex-college professor and had made some kind of a reputation in the concert field as an avantgarde composer, concert pianist, and conductor. James Dean [the star of *East of Eden*] was a piano student of mine, and took Elia Kazan [the director of the film] to a concert I gave at the Museum of Modern Art in New York. Kazan asked me if I would score a film. I knew nothing about movies except that I liked them. When I came on the scene, the big composers in this town were Max Steiner, Dimitri Tiomkin, Bernard Herrmann, and Erich Wolfgang Korngold, who was already dying but was still there.

The kind of music these composers wrote basically had its roots in the nineteenth century with the romantic music of Rachmaninoff, Strauss, Tchaikovsky, Schumann, and Brahms. If, for example, there was a single line in a film, that line was not played by an oboe or a flute; that line was played by all the violins, all the trumpets, all the flutes, all the oboes, and all the clarinets. No one ever took any chances. If you hear a lot of the old scores extracted from the films—which you can today because the soundtrack records are coming back—the music has an incredible thickness to it. It's not a thickness of luster, it's a thickness of turgidity, a lack of profile, a lack of inner voices moving, a lack of counterpoint. It just sounds elephantine.

I remember the first time they recorded *Eden*. I had a solo flute play something and he stopped in the middle and looked around; I said, "What's the problem?" He said, "There isn't anyone playing with me." I said, "No, I'm afraid you have to count." So it became an entirely new development, having a large orchestra but using small chamber ensembles within that orchestra, and using very few entire orchestra sections. You had a curiously different sound in film music. You had much more of a clear focus of the drama, a potentially much greater palette of color in the score. Jack Warner felt rather strange about that because he saw all the orchestra doing nothing, and he didn't like the idea of not having them playing at the same time.

The second film I did at Metro was *The Cobweb*, for John Houseman, who was the producer. Houseman, a very literate man, said he wanted me to write a score of my own style. I said, "Are you sure you know what you're saying?" He said, "Yes, I'll give you carte blanche—do anything you want." I thought the score would be thrown out, but he said, "So be it. I'll fight for it." So I wrote the first twelve-tone score for a major motion picture. At that time Dimitri Mitropoulos was conductor of the New York Philharmonic. He saw the film and asked if I would like to have the sound-track album done by them. I replied that I didn't, because I felt the music was composed for the film. The amount of work it would take to refashion it as a concert piece would be such that I might as well have written a new piece. I don't believe in sound-track albums except as a commercial endeavor.

It was remarkable that I was accepted the way I was and could make a living and try things out. I used films to buy the leisure to write concert music. I used films as a laboratory for dealing with problems. That is not to say I sloughed off writing films, because if your name is on it, you do the best you can. It was a felicitous arrangement because the filmmaker would get something unusual and interesting, and I was able to try out a lot of problem areas in my own work and see what they sounded like. But when I work for a film, my prime objective is to serve the film. Most composers who work in films have a serious problem: they do not write other kinds of music. That means their entire musical ego is tied up in film music. It's very easy to get confused about what kind of music you are writing.

I learned a great deal about music from film, and I learned a great deal about film from music. They're quite similar, simply because they are art devices that move in time and involve the use of the temporal lobe of the brain. That is to say, they involve memory, interpretation, and, more important, they deal with two kinds of time. They deal with real time and psychological time. There may be two pieces of music that are five minutes long; one seems interminable, and the other seems too short. The same with film. One has to know to some degree how one functions with the other in order to become a catalyst for our emotions.

I feel—and this is a statement that might be considered controversial—that music has no emotions at all. Films have emotions because they deal with the pictorialization of emotions that we feel and see and hear about in our everyday experiences. Music is a series of vibrations, of sounds organized rhythmically, that tend to engender emotions in you, but it's the context of the entire thing that causes something to be expressive or inexpressive. It's the context of your experiences and what you bring to the experience of listening to music that makes you feel it as emotional in a certain way.

You'll find two things happening. One, music takes on the protective coloration of the film. If the film is disjunct the music will seem disjunct; if the film is smooth, no matter what the music it will take on this character of the film, because the film is a much stronger stimulus in our society. In Western culture there is nothing more vital in our experience than visual-literary information. The Chinese say that one picture is worth a thousand words. Well, if one picture is worth a thousand words, it most assuredly is worth a million notes. On the other hand, another thing happens reciprocally. The music causes the film to seem slower or faster or smoother or more disjunct in some way. So there's an interaction between the two which influences your perception.

A good case in point is *The Third Man* [Great Britain, 1949, directed by Carol Reed], a film with a great deal of dramatic intensity. There were chases and love scenes and killings and God knows what else; yet the music was one theme played over and over again on one instrument, a zither—a pop tune which became famous at the time [as "The Third Man Theme," by Anton Karas]. Somehow this pop tune, not developed or elaborated but repeated over and over again, took on the same intensity as the scene. It was chase music or love music but it was exactly the same thing.

How do you feel about putting music under dialogue?

ROSENMAN: I generally feel it's not necessary. If the actors are doing a good job—even if they're *not* doing a good job—there's nothing that can help them. If the actors are really doing their stuff, really interacting, that's a kind of chamber music of its own.

You understand the interior monologue and you don't need music. Modern scoring of films involves the listener's being able to hear the music. It used to be that they'd score an entire scene between two actors on the grounds that the scene was dead, that the music would liven it up. You'd ask them what kind of music they wanted, and they'd say something very neutral—and dead. Very often the scene *wasn't* dead, but the filmmaker did not trust his product enough to stand for any kind of silence.

You say music has no emotion. What is it in the final analysis that causes me to say "That didn't work for me emotionally" when I experience the music in relationship to the film?

ROSENMAN: Why something doesn't work and why something appears to work, I think certainly has to do with subjective aspects. But there are certain kinds of underlying precepts which, as a student, one can deal with. The primary factors are consistency and style. The composer for films is really not a note writer; he is a dramatist in his own right, and it is how he sees the dramaturgy or how he sees the mise-en-scène [a French term for direction— literally, "placement in the scene"—generally used in filmmaking to connote meaningful use of screen space] musically—in its larger sense—that determines whether something is going to work. What the composer is trying to say along with the filmmaker should in some way achieve the same consistency. Now, the consistency may not be literally what the filmmaker is talking about. Ideally speaking, the composer should make you see something in that film that you couldn't have seen without the music. The music enters the plot directly.

For example, you have an opening shot, which you've seen many times, I'm sure—a helicopter shot of New York. This helicopter goes down into the canyons of New York, and you see people rushing around, cars; it goes smack into the so-called concrete jungle. You have several options with the sound track. You have the option of having it silent, which would create a certain kind of mood. You have the option of the sound effects of the city, which would be a kind of realism, a documentary style. You have the option of writing the kind of big-city music you used to hear in the old films, a lot of xylophones, à la Gershwin, musical sound effects which don't really add to anything you've seen on the screen except reinforce it to some degree.

Then you might have another idea. Suppose the filmmaker says, "Is there any way for the music to say that the city, for all its tremendous crowds, is a very lonely place?" If the composer took a lonely saxophone line with a lot of echo and played a long, slow, plaintive tune against this terrific mélange, you would get an idea of the city you couldn't have gotten without that sound track. In other words, the sound track would tell you something about the scene that the image itself couldn't tell you. This, in my estimation, is the role of music in movies.

It has to do with the communication between the filmmaker and the composer. The composer has to be interested enough to get into the film at the very beginning, before the script has even jelled. Generally film composers are not that interested; it takes too much time and they don't make enough money. Step two, if the scriptwriter knows enough about music to understand its nature and its relationship to the drama he's creating, if he can say, "I think the music can take the place of the written word in this scene"—if he can do that, a real collaboration begins. It would seem to me that the only way to communicate between a filmmaker and a composer is verbally, and that is extremely imprecise. The only advice I can offer to all potential filmmakers in regard to working with a composer—and I have to resort to the language of the young—is that the vibes have to be very good. There has to be a sense of trust. There has to be a mutual understanding of what the music is trying to say in the film. That's the most important consideration.

The filmmaker should know something about music and what music can do, or else be modest enough to ask "Can music do this?" rather than tell me what music can do. I think most people who are making films know absolutely nothing about music.

The next question is, "Well, *what* can music do?" If he understands his film, he will ipso facto understand the components of the film—that is, music. Kazan understood his film and what he wanted to say with it. On *East of Eden* I went along on location; I wrote the scenes while the film was being shot. I worked with Kazan right from the first day of shooting. And when the film was rough-cut the music was rough-cut. I played the music for the actors before they went out to do their scenes. In scenes where the music carries forth the rhythm of the scene rather than the dialogue, Kazan let me dictate the action of the scene by directing it with me like an opera. To my amazement, he said that he had often wanted to work like that. That's ideal.

Would you talk about sound effects?

ROSENMAN: When I say "sound track" I don't mean only music, I mean the sound of film as being part of the whole communication. Kazan said I should take over the administration of the entire sound of *East of Eden*—bird sounds, footfalls—and should supervise the dubbing, so that the entire style of the film was consistent. That included finding out whether the actor was a bass, a soprano, or a tenor, and scoring accordingly, or dubbing somebody's footfalls if you wanted that as part of the rhythm. Or silence. And that meant *silence*, nothing, no sound at all. The real filmmakers aren't afraid of those kinds of things.

I've tried some odd things. For example, I once recorded a bunch of people speaking like we're talking now and put it through a very heavy echo chamber so that you couldn't understand the words. I used that in a suspense scene. It was terrific. A composer should try a dramaturgic solution.

When I was working in theater we occasionally took arbitrary pieces of film and put them together with pieces of music that had no rational connection. The results were often fantastic. Is that of value to you as a composer?

ROSENMAN: It's of value in an experimental sense. It's of value if you learn something from it. But I think that the dereliction of control in art makes it less art. I'm not saying there's no place for improvisation, because, after all, jazz and all popular music are based on improvisation, and I adore improvisational theater if it's really done well. But I think the more control the artist has over his material, the closer to art it is.

In film it really seems to me that the more toward art it is, the more of a one-man show it is. You take the great filmmakers of all time—Fellini and Bergman, people of that kind—and you know damn well that there's no decision being made by committee in those films. They are the final arbiters of taste in their films. I know Fellini quite well because I lived in Italy for four years, and even in the scoring sessions Fellini is in complete control. It's his film; he knows what he wants. The idea of the compartmentalization of art may perfect it in some sense, but it perfects it in terms of industry and not in terms of art. I just don't think the twain can meet. Of course you can say, "The Sistine Chapel was made by seventy people who worked for Michelangelo." But Michelangelo dictated every brush stroke.

When you work in television, are you pretty much on your own?
ROSENMAN: In series television there's absolutely no input. I did *Marcus Welby* for six years, which would make me either the healthiest man in the world or the sickest, depending on how you look at it. After the second year I was all alone; I'd record and never see the show again. I'd score about thirteen shows and the other twenty-six they'd track from that. It was all disease music, and I literally saw a brain-operation score become a mastectomy score. Television is the quintessential schlock medium. All scores in television are modular units, wallpaper. I defy anybody to find the basic difference, musically, between the main title for one series and another series. They all have bongo drums and sound like be-bop of the '40s.

How do you go about spotting a film [picking the spots for the music]?
ROSENMAN: I prefer to see the film before it's finished so that I can get some ideas. For a major feature film they spend about a year, and then the composer comes in and is given about four weeks to match this conception, which I think is unfair and generally doesn't give the filmmaker his money's worth. It's ideal for the composer to have as much communication as he can with the filmmaker. When I spot a film I try to see the film as often as I can, and then I'll sit down with the filmmaker and we'll run the film on a stop-go projector; I'll say, "Well, I think music should do this and that. I think it should go from here to there." Sometimes there'll be questions or arguments: "I don't think it needs it there" or "Well, I would like to say so-and-so there." Let's say that a man and woman are kissing: "I'd like to show the poisonous element in this in some way because three reels later he kills her." In other words, we talk about dramaturgy. We also find out where we can orchestrate with silence.

It's very important for the composer to know what music *can't* do. I did a main title for a series that became a tremendous hit, *The Defenders*. The guy in charge, a very bright guy, said, "I'd like the music to express the law." I said, "Well, music can't express the law. It's not possible. If you want the music to express majesty or something like that, it will only express majesty if what you have on the screen is majestic." Music can't open and shut doors. National General called me once and asked me to save a picture. I said, "Yes, if I can reshoot it with different actors and a different script, by all means." Because most filmmakers don't understand music, they feel it has the power to heal, to cure broken legs, to cure stuttering, to cure bad photography, bad acting. I'm sorry to say that it can't do any of that. It's up to you. You have to do good films; then the music will appear better too.

What if you're having trouble communicating with the director? How do you work then?

ROSENMAN: You simply have to hope the guy is going to trust you enough to leave you alone. Because most filmmakers are terribly afraid. They don't know whether it's good or bad. I've known a lot of filmmakers over the past twenty years. Some of them are very literate, but they all seem to have no communication with music at all. They've never been to a concert. They don't listen to classical music on records. I'm not saying they should listen to classical music as opposed to popular music, but I think they should familiarize themselves with that kind of stuff too. I probably know as much popular music as they do, but they don't know anything of what *I* know. This is a product of their lack of imagination, even with regard to film. It's like a person who says to me, "Well, I'll tell you, I don't like avant-garde music. Just give me Beethoven." I would maintain that that person really doesn't understand Beethoven.

You did an eighteenth-century score for Barry Lyndon *[1975, directed by Stanley Kubrick]. How much did you steep yourself in that tradition? And how much of a perfectionist was Kubrick in terms of what he asked you to do?*

ROSENMAN: Well, first of all, Stanley called me on a Monday and said to come to England on Wednesday—the picture was finished. He said he had all the music picked out and all I had to do was arrange it. They told me Stanley worked this way, and, frankly, I wanted a trip to England. I had never done an adaptation before, and it gave me a chance to conduct the London Orchestra with some classical pieces I was interested in. I was under no illusions that I had any creative work to do on the film.

I asked him what he had picked out and he said, "The first thing I want to do is to buy the theme from *The Godfather*." I said, "Well, if you're going to do that, tell me now so I can get the first plane out of England." "What's wrong with it? It's a very beautiful theme." I said, "You're right, but the last time I saw *The Godfather*, it was about gangsters, not eighteenth-century aristocrats." I listened to all the records he had, and he had picked a sarabande which had been recorded with a harpsichord; he thought the bass would just be marvelous for the duel scenes. He had another theme for the dying child, which was from one of Verdi's worst operas. It was as though a psych class had gotten together and said, "Let's find something that will really repel people." I told him I couldn't go along with that and suggested I do an arrangement of the tune for strings, continuo, harpsichord, and percussion, and see what it sounded like. We tried it with the London Symphony and he fell madly in love with it.

I left after having picked out all the music and recorded it there. He then practically made a loop out of the Verdi theme and used it over and over again. If I had known he wanted that much of it, I would have orchestrated some other variations; there were five charming variations in that piece. When I saw the film I saw this incredibly boring film with all the music I had picked out going over and over again. I thought, "My God, what a mess!" I was going to refuse the Oscar. The classical music used in the film is much closer to me, because I am a pianist. I was a Bach and Haydn specialist. I picked out about half of it and he picked out about half.

What is the weakest point of these auteurs' films? The photography in all these films is marvelous. The mise-en-scène is fantastic, the performances are often breathtaking. The only thing they lack is any kind of story. Don't tell me that Bob Altman's specialty is story, because if it is, he's in serious trouble. The European directors are able to take an idea and develop it.

We in the United States don't see the difference between the following things: motion and emotion, freedom and aimlessness, development and repetition. To be able to perceive the difference between any of these, you have to be reasonably mature. A function of maturity is memory and education. I don't mean formal education necessarily, but an ability to learn. I've never found the ability to learn present in any of these directors. All I found was a colossal ego which covered a terrible sense of emptiness. The problem with the American auteur is that he gets too much too fast. They're failing upward, which is destroying their sense of self-criticism. In addition, these filmmakers are so zealous about controlling every part of the film and not trusting—a lot of them are strange, paranoid kinds of guys—that they use records or source music. They will trade off flexibility for control. Their ego really gets in the way of creative impulses.

The good composers, the ones with a real sense of dramaturgy, would probably be as good if not better filmmakers than most of the filmmakers they work for, because they have a real understanding of many aspects of life and art, which filmmakers don't. It's important for filmmakers to know painting, literature, music, because filmmaking is a marriage of all those arts in the twentieth century. A filmmaker can't simply be a director or a cinematographer anymore. If he wants to be an artist he has to know everything.

I'm saying a lot of things here, but among them is that one should have a sense of adventure. That's the important thing.

THE PRODUCTION DESIGNER
Polly·Platt

One of the new breed of Hollywood production designers who take responsibility not only for the sets but for the overall look of a film, Polly Platt has carved out a strong independent reputation as a designer and also as a screenwriter since her initial films with her ex-husband, director Peter Bogdanovich.

She co-wrote and designed the first film Bogdanovich directed, the underrated 1968 thriller *Targets*. Their unusually close, almost symbiotic, partnership soared with the black-and-white 1950s nostalgia piece, *The Last Picture Show*, the pop-art comedy *What's Up, Doc?*, and the bittersweet Depression-era comedy-drama *Paper Moon*.

Platt had a deep influence on all aspects of these Bogdanovich films, from the selection of the material through the writing and casting to the shooting and editing. Since 1974 their careers have gone separate ways, and Platt has continued as a successful production designer on such films as *The Bad News Bears* and *A Star Is Born* while also making a name for herself as a screenwriter with the controversial Louis Malle film about child prostitution, *Pretty Baby*.

Asked once to define the role of a production designer, Platt

127

said, "The production designer, as I'm called, usually establishes the look of a film, the visual carrying out of the themes within a script. I always do both the production design and the costumes; I think one person should do both. The set designer is, in essence, an architect. The production designer makes a drawing of what he wants and the set designer puts it into blueprint. He points out what you might need to make a set structurally sound. Generally speaking, the look of the film is my concept."

Born in the late 1930s, Platt was raised on Army posts around the country. Originally intending to be a painter, she later became interested in the theater. She attended Carnegie Tech in Pittsburgh, but when she was told that a woman could not be a scenic designer, she left after a year studying costuming.

She met Bogdanovich, with whom she shared a passionate interest in films, while both were active in summer stock. He had established a reputation as a journalist and film scholar before they moved to Hollywood in 1964. His work on several Roger Corman films led to Corman's giving him the chance to direct *Targets*, which started both Bogdanovich's and Platt's careers.

In the last few years Platt has concentrated on screenwriting because of the demands of raising her two children, but she recently designed another film, Steve Martin's horror spoof *The Man with Two Brains*. She has had offers to direct but so far has not opted to do so.

FILMOGRAPHY

1968 *Targets* (also writer)   1970–75 *The Other Side of the Wind* (uncompleted)   1971 *The Last Picture Show*   1972 *What's Up, Doc?*   1974 *Paper Moon* / *The Thief Who Came to Dinner* 1976 *The Bad News Bears* / *A Star Is Born*   1977 *Pretty Baby* (writer only)   1979 *Good Luck, Miss Wyckoff* (writer only) 1983 *The Man with Two Brains*

THE SEMINAR

Polly Platt held a seminar with the Fellows of the Center for Advanced Film Studies on December 7, 1977.

What was your training?
PLATT: I went to Carnegie Tech to study scenic design in the theater. Because I was a girl, and because you were required to lift the scenery on the stage, they wouldn't let me study or work in the shop. Nobody really thought of it as discrimination at the time—they really just didn't think a woman could do the work. So I quit and went to New York, where I started working for free doing scenery in summer stock. I haven't lifted anything in a number of years, not even my children.

The first film set I ever did was on *Targets,* in 1968. I didn't know anything. And to save money I had to build one set which would change into another: Boris Karloff's hotel room had to change into the murderer's whole house. I designed the set and drew the elevations. The only problem was that I never measured the size of the stage, and my set was ten feet bigger than the stage. It didn't fit. When they started to put it up—you know, they pre-fabbed the walls—they got to a certain part of the wall and there just was no more stage left. Nothing. And everybody came running to me. They thought *they* had made a mistake! We had to cut some walls right in half, just shove them together. I learned to measure the stage before I put the set on it. I was lucky to be able to work the way I hope all of you work, which is do low-budget films and work, just do a lot of work.
Could you talk about your contribution to The Last Picture Show?
PLATT: Well, I was married to Peter [Bogdanovich, the director] then, and I would say it was a very collaborative effort. Sal Mineo had given me the novel by Larry McMurtry three years before we made it. We have Sal to thank for that movie. I loved the book and made a note of it. It's very much Peter's film.

As a designer, I had to find the right locations and pay attention to the period. I used *I Love Lucy,* those old '50s comedy shows, to evoke that period for me. What was interesting was shooting in black and white. Naturally, we had planned to make a color picture. Orson Welles and Larry McMurtry kept saying, "We think it should be in black and white." Bert Schneider, who financed the film, really backed us up on that after he checked with the exhibitors, who said it made no difference to them. And I think that's what made the film.

Did you have certain painters or photographers in mind for the look of the film?

PLATT: No. What I had in mind was the photography of the Warners pictures in the '40s. I thought the picture was a little gray, but it looks good. The only strong visual theme was desolation. The landscape where we made the film, in north-central Texas, is so desolate. We tried to use the high horizon—in other words, small land with big sky. For us the land was a character.

What sets did you build?

PLATT: A lot. The cafe; the front of the main street. But the pool hall was just sitting there. I didn't touch it. I didn't even wash the windows. And that's another important thing about art direction: knowing when to do something, and when not to; when not to say "I know how to do it better." The pool hall was perfect. It was really a domino parlor; I put the pool tables in. It was so old that the paint was hanging off the ceiling; it looked like bats. I was told that the men who used the hall smoked, and the paint had peeled off, so the nicotine had stained the ceiling with all that brown fuzz. I said to the cinematographer, Bob Surtees, "Now, I'm just going to scrape the ceiling and paint it, and it'll be fine." I'll never forget the expression on his face. I was joking with him, you know, because it had so much character.

Have you ever considered doing a film that offered a lot of possibilities for design and creative work, even though it didn't come together as a story?

PLATT: No. I don't think you should do a script because of visual possibilities, only if you like the script, the story. Also, nobody should really be aware of the sets, unless we are talking about a cartoon like *What's Up, Doc?* where you are fooling around. On *Paper Moon*, or *The Last Picture Show*, or *A Star Is Born*, or any film about which you feel serious at all, your work should be invisible. I've always thought that I was more conceptually involved in design than I was an architect. I always hate design which makes you feel the designer is showing off.

So then your job, essentially, is to take the director's concept and extend it into visuals. You've got to have a pretty good relationship with the director.

PLATT: You sure do. And sometimes you work with directors who don't have any visual concepts.

So you have to create it for them?

PLATT: Well, you have to create it for *yourself*. Everybody is always saying you have to make the director feel it's his idea; I don't agree. I think you should present what you think, how you think the film should look, to the director. If he doesn't agree, you should consult, and then he lets you do it your way, and that's the way it should be.

But I always find directors talking to me about how they want a "look" like Vermeer and Rembrandt, and all of a sudden when we start shooting they don't remember anything. Or the cinematographer wants a diffused, gray tone to the film. He'll say, "We won't shoot on a sunny day. Never. We want it gloomy, dark, and we don't want any contrast in this film." Then a sunny day will arrive and we'll have nothing to shoot, and all of a sudden we're shooting. Because what can you do? It's called money. It costs money to achieve style, and it requires great innovative abilities.

How long before a picture shoots are you hired?

PLATT: Three to four months. And they pay me, too!

Do you then work with the location person?

PLATT: I go there myself. I don't know of any good production designer or art director who doesn't. Usually when I come on a film, people let me do what I want. On *A Star Is Born*, Barbra Streisand and Jon Peters [the producer] backed me up. They never even saw the Arizona location. The end of *A Star Is Born* was originally set in a house next to the ocean, just like in the original movies. I said, "Oh, God, you just can't do this. *Won Ton Ton* is being made with a dog going into the ocean [in a spoof of the famous *Star Is Born* ending]." I know Arizona very well, because I lived down there where they let me build that house. They had confidence.

How did you approach What's Up, Doc?

PLATT: I looked at all of Barbra's films. I wanted to do something different. I thought that she was always dressed too eccentrically; and I thought, where could we set her where she wouldn't be so New York Jewish? I decided *What's Up, Doc?* was a cartoon. That's why I tried to make her clothes very "unclothesy." I went from New York to Chicago to Denver to Houston, looking for a city for her. When I saw San Francisco it seemed to be a white city. The chase sequences weren't in yet. All that was later written by Buck Henry after I picked San Francisco. Peter loved the idea.

I didn't believe in Barbra as a real character, and I didn't believe anything in the film—none of that could really happen; so that was the theme of the film visually. It was mainly that everywhere this girl went there was destruction. Then the color: we tried to keep it black and white. Peter was the kind of director who encouraged finding a style and sticking to it.

In one of the sets, the home of the young millionaire played by Austin Pendleton, you had a very striking see-through staircase.

PLATT: In the old movies, the people who had money were always old and had great mahogany libraries with leather seats and all that. I just didn't think I could make a set like that; it's so old-fashioned. Young people are in control of money now. I felt that Austin's character was a pretentious, transparent rich guy. So I made everything plexiglass—plexiglass staircase, plexiglass pillars. Since it was San Francisco and there were those beautiful narrow Victorian gingerbread houses, I thought what better example of the bad taste of the nouveau riche than to take a beautiful Victorian house, rip out the inside, and put in plexiglass? That was built on the stage to the dimensions of a real house in San Francisco. It was all just a literal translation of my interpretation of the character. That's also why I dressed him all in white.

Peter just loved the set. When he saw it, he changed the script. He decided to stage the whole fight around the staircase. He got an idea for a shot—to show the face of the man right through the staircase, a complete cartoon idea. And Peter hates ugly feet, so, as a joke, at one end of the set I had this abstract painting of an ugly foot. This was again the taste of the young millionaire played by Austin Pendleton. Peter saw it and laughed. He knew why I had put it up there. He said, "Wouldn't it be great if somebody shot a gun, the picture broke loose, and the 'foot' came down and kicked somebody in the head?" We did it.

So it was a classic example of perfect artistic cooperation. I designed a set and the director was inspired and used the set. By the way, the set cost $250,000, the most expensive set I ever built. *For the set of Kris Kristofferson's home in* A Star Is Born, *did you base it on any one house, or did you go around to a lot of rock stars' homes?*

PLATT: I went to a lot of rock stars' homes. I didn't have any idea how those people lived. I found out a lot of them live in motor homes. One house looked like a gauche nouveau riche house on Long Island, with purple rugs and gold banisters. All these superstars live differently from what you would expect.

I would have liked to have done something different with Kris's house, and I lost on that one. I would've liked him to live in the San Fernando Valley, in a more bourgeois, simple house which had been converted into a music studio—not the mansion. The only guy whose house was a little bit like that was Leon Russell. His house has wall-to-wall carpeting, right up the wall and onto the ceiling, because his living room is his recording studio. That's where I got the idea.

My idea about Kris's house was that everything about Kris should be dark and black, deep, dark tones: *depressing.* And everything about Barbra should be white, light, so that when they got together it should be a smashing contrast, which again was conceptual.

When you look for locations, who has the final say?

PLATT: It's the same old question. Sometimes the studio has the final say, although most of the time they will listen to us. On *Pretty Baby* [which Platt wrote but did not design], you would imagine that they would listen to director Louis Malle and myself. No. They didn't want us to go to New Orleans; they want you to shoot in Los Angeles because it's cheaper. Every single film is a different decision. Sometimes there's no argument because it's so major it *has* to be in a certain location.

What will usually cinch it is somebody who's sympathetic— somebody like David Picker [then a Paramount executive], who helped so much on *Pretty Baby,* who understands your artistic needs, even though it may cost more money. We found a house in New Orleans, which we got for $9,000 for the whole shooting schedule. I couldn't have built the set in Hollywood for $550,000. We had the expense of taking everybody on location, but we saved on that single location. And I wrote the movie to be cheap. I wrote it all in one set, essentially, even though there are four or five other small locations.

Is the budget established before you start? Do you establish the budget?

PLATT: That's another game, a ridiculous game, and there is no beating that one. When I first got into pictures, I didn't understand anything about why everybody was so uptight about budgets. On *Paper Moon* I went over budget on one set. There is a little set, a general store where Tatum O'Neal pulls a scam. I was $3,000 over budget because I had to build that whole set. It was a burned-out building; I picked it because of the reverse—out the window there was a *real* period-looking [1930s] street, and I liked being able to see people going up and down the street. I knew the way Peter would shoot out the window, and I knew Laszlo Kovacs, the cinematographer, would balance the light so that it wouldn't flare out and you could see what was out there. I went over budget and everybody got so excited. Everybody started having meetings. I found out that production budgets each set, and it doesn't matter that you are $4,000 under budget on the set before, it only matters that you are $3,000 over budget on *this* set.

Do you stick to the budget you submit?

PLATT: Now I ignore it completely, because it's a game. But as a production designer you do your very best to do it as inexpensively as possible. To go over budget gets you a bad reputation—unless you get Oscars. Of course, you submit your budget and you know what you want. If they push you down, then you begin to eliminate. Sometimes you have to eliminate some of your most innovative ideas because no one wants to spend the money. You can't build four plain walls now in a studio for less than $75,000 to $100,000. It doesn't matter what size set it is. I'm talking about Barbra Streisand's apartment in *A Star Is Born*—that little tiny thing? That was $95,000, undressed. Four walls. I was shocked. So you learn. That's working in a studio. That's why you like to go on location. You get it for free. You pay $100 a day for a real location for one week.

Do you design the costumes for your projects, as well as the scenery?

PLATT: With the exception of *A Star Is Born*, where I did not do Barbra's costumes.

Does a production designer usually design the costumes?
PLATT: Usually a production designer does not. I am the only one I know of who does design the costumes, except for Cecil Beaton, who did *My Fair Lady*. It's all a question of who has more guts, who has more clout with the director, who can outwit—you know, if you think you are *right*. The director is the only person who can help you in a situation like that. The sets, for me, are totally dictated by the characters. So therefore the clothes the characters wear have to be related to where they live.

When I went to the movies, I used to think, "These clothes don't have anything to do with these characters. What is this tailored suit doing on every person Edith Head designs for? Why does everybody look like a *Vogue* magazine person? Why don't people design the clothes to match the people? Why is Sophia Loren wearing these weird clothes when she is supposed to be somebody else?" I remember that *Charade* drove me crazy. Audrey Hepburn in those Paris fashions—she wasn't a real person at all. And I thought, "This character is a person who doesn't care about anything except buying her clothes in Paris." It hurt the film. I always thought the men's clothes fit too well. Clothes *don't* fit correctly. What's funnier than a guy with the shoulders down, or the sleeves too short? I think that is character. Character comes out of design, or vice versa, and that's why I think I must have the total say-so.

That's how I got fired by [director] Mike Nichols from *The Fortune*: for trying too hard to get it my way, the way that was right for the film—casting, locations, script. It's important for somebody to stand up for style and integrity. You can become very unpopular, and I have a reputation for being a very unpleasant person, a "ballsy chick." But I think it's worth it. Then the people who really want you around will learn to appreciate you. I'm too outspoken and too talkative, and maybe I'm overprotective of the need to be able to speak your mind, because this is a town that's frightening. I have been frightened. I have been told that I would never work again because I talk too much and give my opinion too much. I think if you are not allowed to, then what is real within you will be destroyed.

How much do you have to be a "ballsy chick" to make it? Would you have made it if you were a "yes girl"?

PLATT: I don't think that I would have gotten anywhere if I had been a "yes girl." And I don't think I have to work harder than anybody else to make it, a man or a woman. I consider myself an artist first, sex is second. I'm not antifeminist, or profeminist, or antimale. It's very, very difficult to balance the strength of your opinion. You are working with some people who have more experience than you. A lot of times you just don't know when to back down, you just don't know when you are wrong, and you really have to sit there and listen. But you have to be strong or by the time they finish with you it's garbage.

How did you approach designing the baseball field for The Bad News Bears?

PLATT: That was just a joke. I got into the most trouble, being a woman, on that picture. They said, "Why did you hire a woman to design a *baseball field?*" But there's nothing easier in the world. You just go get the Little League baseball guide, a little book that tells you exactly how to do it.

What is it like being constantly on the set, involved in the production of a film you've written?

PLATT: You mean like *Pretty Baby?* It's a brand-new experience, and it's one of the most painful experiences I've ever had, one of the most frustrating. I did not design the picture. I don't want to design anymore; it isn't that I don't like it, it's that I've always wanted to be a writer, and I have two children in desperate need of me. They are very small, and I can't go away for months at a time anymore. I just have to change my life.

Could you speak about some of the frustrations on Pretty Baby?

PLATT: We'd be here another four hours. I've spent most of my life now on sets, it seems. You don't know when to get out of the way, you don't know when to stop insisting and let the movie take place in the hands and mind of the *now* creator—Louis, in this case. I don't think it is wise for a writer to go on the set. The problem is that the writer is a second-class citizen at that point. You're really nobody. You have to understand that writers are a neglected aspect of Hollywood society—that if you are a writer, you are going to be miserable. You're just going to have to realize that's the way it is, because the director gets all the credit. And in a sense, he deserves it. If you get up there and try it sometime, you'll see why he gets it. I don't think anybody should be bitter.

There's just too much money. Really. If you don't understand that, if you can't take it, then find something else to do.

Would you like to direct?

PLATT: I have not planned to direct, and I'm not being coy. I'm scared of it. If I feel impelled to direct a film, I will. If I write a picture that I feel only I can direct, I will do it. That would be it for me, and I would be happy to do it. I've always said I won't, because I've always wanted to be a writer. It sounds odd, but I feel that design is an extension of writing, or writing is an extension of design, whichever way you want to put it.

THE EDITOR
Verna Fields

Verna Fields, who died in 1982, was fondly known as "Mother Cutter" to the young directors with whom she preferred to work. Her editing as well as her advice in all areas of filmmaking were acknowledged as crucial to the success of such key 1970s films as Peter Bogdanovich's *What's Up, Doc?* and *Paper Moon*, George Lucas's *American Graffiti*, and Steven Spielberg's *Jaws*, for which she won an Academy Award.

Because of her work on *Jaws*, Fields was rewarded by Universal Pictures with the position of executive consultant, and in 1976 she became feature production vice-president. She was later given the additional responsibility of liaison between filmmakers and the distribution department, and during her seven years at Universal she was regarded as one of the most influential women in Hollywood.

Born in St. Louis in 1918, Fields was the daughter of screenwriter and former newspaperman Sam Hellman (*Little Miss Marker, My Darling Clementine*). After receiving a journalism degree from the University of Southern California, she worked as a reader at 20th Century-Fox before becoming an assistant sound editor on Fritz Lang's *The Woman in the Window* (1944). On that film she met her future husband, editor Sammy Fields; after a four-year apprenticeship, she left the business to raise a family, returning after her husband's death in 1954. She spent several years as a sound editor on the TV series *Sky King* and *Death Valley Days* and on such features as *El Cid* (for which she won the American Cinema Editors' award), *The Balcony*, and Peter Bogdanovich's directing debut, *Targets*.

Fields's first feature-film editing credit was on Irving Lerner's *Studs Lonigan* in 1960. During the mid-1960s she edited a number of independent films, including *Nothing But a Man*, *The Bus*, and *Deathwatch*. From 1965 to 1970 she edited, produced, and directed documentaries for U.S. government agencies and taught advanced film editing at USC.

Bogdanovich lured her back to feature films with *What's Up, Doc?* in 1972. It was an enormous commercial success, as was her next film, *American Graffiti*, for which she received an Oscar nomination. She edited Spielberg's first feature, *The Sugarland Express*, and when *Jaws* ran into serious production problems, Fields provided a creative and personal anchor for the young director. Although she often denied having "saved" the film, others have paid her that accolade.

After Fields became an executive at Universal, studio production chief Ned Tanen publicly offered her a chance to direct, but she never found a property that interested her sufficiently to lure her away from her favorite role as a director's counselor and troubleshooter.

FILMOGRAPHY

1960 *Studs Lonigan* / *The Savage Eye*   1961 *El Cid* (sound editor)   1963 *An Affair of the Skin* / *Cry of Battle* / *The Balcony* (sound editor)   1964 *Nothing But a Man*   1965 *The Bus*   1966 *Country Boy* / *Deathwatch*   1967 *Legend of the Boy and the Eagle*   1968 *Track of Thunder* / *The Wild Racers* / *Targets* (sound editor)   1969 *Medium Cool*   1972 *What's Up, Doc?*   1973 *American Graffiti*   1974 *Paper Moon* / *Daisy Miller* / *The Sugarland Express*   1975 *Jaws*

THE SEMINAR

Verna Fields held a seminar with the Fellows of the Center for Advanced Film Studies on December 3, 1975.

You've worked with a number of the most important young directors in the industry today. They all seem to have a very strong concern for being in total control of the editing of their films. Are they more difficult to work with than directors used to be?

FIELDS: No, because I think they *should* be in control. Maybe that's why I like working with them. The idea of an editor's having control over a director's work is ludicrous. I wish the word "editing" had never been invented; people feel there is some kind of friction between the director and the editor, because the word "editing" implies correcting, and it's not. In French, the word is *monteur*, which is what it is; you're mounting the film.

Now, you need to be damn creative and intelligent to do it well, and you can come up with some great creative ideas. I'm enormously proud of a lot of pictures I've done. By God, I saved the picture, and I've been given credit for it. I don't think that my creative input has ever been denied by the fact that the director has complete control. It's his picture: he shot it, conceived it. In the final analysis you are answerable to the man who put up the money, but if he hires a director to make a film for him, then he must let that director make his film.

How does an editor work with the director?

FIELDS: Every editor works a little differently, so I can only speak for myself: I work very closely with the director. I'll climb inside the director's head if he'll let me. I think it's just a fiasco when the editor is not near production; I see no way at all for the editor to know what the director is trying to do. Hopefully, the director has in mind how he wants the picture cut; he's visualizing the picture together, not just little shots. I don't like to cut a picture twice; I don't want to cut a picture my way and his way—I want to cut it his way. If I have different ideas, though, I want to argue with him. I'm terribly stubborn; I fight.

So you're on the set all the time?

FIELDS: If there's a certain scene I'm confused about, then I want to be on the set. I like to talk to the director in advance; I like to know how he plans on shooting it. I can tell from the way he's staging it and the way he's talking what he has in mind. There are times directors say, "Oh, my God, I'm lost, so I shot every angle in sight. Do something." Then you go to work and you do something. But basically I don't think the editor's work is separate from the director's.

How do you handle disagreements?

FIELDS: The first thing I do is tell the director that there's no way he can't win. I don't think I've ever had a director refuse to let me try something. I've gone so far as to make a dupe [a duplicate work print] on something if it's terribly complex and if I'm sure I'm right and he's going to make me do it another way. I'll say, "Fine. Let me get a dupe so I don't have to rework it all in case you find out I'm right." I'm not going to go behind his back; I'm not going to do anything to hurt him in any way, and I'm not going to be destructive with his picture. He has to know that I'm trying my damnedest—for the picture, really, not him, the man.

What is your involvement on the set?

FIELDS: Just watching and listening, although I'm not the kind of person who keeps quiet if I see something. It makes my work very easy if I know what the director is trying to do. If I can see that he's trying to pull a certain something from an actor and I see that on take three he got it and kept on going and then on take five he quit, I still know that what he saw on take three was what he liked, but it was also the camera movement on take five. Maybe I can accomplish being on take three for the moment but still get to take five for the move.

It's pretty hard for him when he comes to dailies [daily screenings during production of the unedited footage] to remember all those things. If I'm there and know what's going on I remember a lot of them. It just saves me time. We might be sitting around waiting for lighting and we start talking about the scene. The director says, "This is a very important scene in the picture." "Why?" "Because this is the scene in which I really want to show that she's starting to miss him, that she's thinking about him." Well, I can tell that he's going to want some lingering cuts on her.

Steven Spielberg is wonderful [Fields cut *The Sugarland Express* and *Jaws* for Spielberg]. You're on the set and somebody will make a suggestion. He'll say, "Boy, terrific." He'll go over and start to set it up and say, "Got a better idea yet," and he'll go from there. He's very receptive; he has no ego problems.

Other people are very firm; they come on the set knowing exactly what they want to do and how they want to do it and they don't want to hear anything. There are a lot of cutters, prop men, set designers, and cameramen who would blow a fuse at a director who changes his mind after they've got all their chalk marks on the floor. I think a well-prepared but fluid man at the helm is about the best there is.

What is the daily routine for an editor during production?

FIELDS: You usually get the dailies in the morning; an assistant will synch them up [match sound with picture]; I like to look at them then, assuming that I have not been on the set the day before, so that when I finally do see the director, who may have very little time, I will have studied it in advance. Possibly the producers will see it at noon or maybe the company breaks at noon and sees it and the director doesn't see it until the end of the day. In any event, a list is made up with the scene numbers, and when I have enough material to fill out a whole scene I will start cutting it.

Probably the next day I will try to snag the director and talk to him about the sequence I cut. I'll say, "It went together magnificently, just the way you shot it" or "I had a bit of trouble with such-and-such. Do you want to see it?" There are times when a director will say to me, "Please don't cut that sequence until we have the time to look at it closely. I have some really crazy ideas that you couldn't know by the way I shot it, but I realized afterward that I wanted to do something different." So I'll leave it intact and that's the way it goes. Pretty soon a sequence becomes a reel and a reel becomes half a film and eventually a whole film.

There are other ways of doing it. There are some people who assemble, just cut off the slates [scene beginning and end markers] and do it that way in master shots [shots covering entire scenes, which are later combined with close-ups and other shots]. I think eventually you get a reputation for working a certain way and directors hire you because that's the way they want to work.

We have heard that the sequence of the boat chasing the shark in Jaws *was restructured on the editing table. Could you explain that?*

FIELDS: There are a lot of misconceptions about what happened on *Jaws*, partially because when a picture is that hot everybody is interviewed, and there are a lot of crazy stories. What actually happened was that I got very busy, so I wasn't even cutting then. There was no way we could ever finish the picture in the time we had. Steven Spielberg sent me out to do some second-unit work [scenes shot by another director and crew, usually of action, special effects, or other time-consuming elements not involving principal cast members], and because the script girl couldn't be on the boat with him due to space constraints, there were tremendous mixups in scene numbers and continuity. So what I decided to do was to assemble the dailies as best we could in a cutting continuity. I would get Steve to come up once in a while and look at dailies, and he'd say, "Oh, no, no. That barrel going that way I stole for that sequence over there." It was really kind of a game; it was like a jigsaw puzzle.

When we came back from Martha's Vineyard [the island location in Massachusetts] almost every sequence in the picture was cut except for the chase. So we went to the cutting room, which is at my house, and we sat at the Kem [an editing machine with small viewing screens] and looked at it in complete order. We discussed the way we thought it should go and picked takes. There were enormous problems with matching the look of water, sky, things like that. But we suddenly realized that the picture really worked. There were some cuts I would have liked to make that we didn't, because the continuity just looked too bad, but if we managed to distract the eye for a moment with action we could make it work. A lot of correction work can be done in the lab, and you can live with some bad lighting. After it's cut it works; it doesn't really bother you. The sky in *Jaws* didn't bother you. Lighting has never hampered me as much as angles have.

There was a lot of talk on the set that if *Jaws* ever got together it would be a miracle, and the picture would never get to the screen unless Verna was a genius. It isn't true. But no one really knew what pieces were going to be put in where; it was so mixed up because they were so dependent on weather and special effects and whether the shots worked that day. When I direct it's not going to be a special-effects picture.

Since you started editing, younger directors have become much more unconventional with their use of camera movements. Has that affected your editing?

FIELDS: When a director gets into creative camera movements he'd better know what he's doing because, boy, can you get screwed up. I get very annoyed sometimes when I see a picture where camera movement is used arbitrarily and is overdone. I don't like to be aware of the cameraman. I don't like to be aware of any of the technical things when I'm seeing a movie unless it's for a purpose. Arbitrary moves and rack focuses [abrupt changes of focal emphasis] drive me crazy. There are very few of them that have been subtle enough to work for me. As far as I'm concerned, the play is the thing. First comes the writer. When I say that it is up to the editor to put together what the director has shot, I feel just as strongly that it is up to the director to direct what the writer wrote.

How do you maintain objectivity when you're editing?

FIELDS: It is something some people have and some people haven't. I don't think I have a problem in being objective, but there are occasions when I'm proven wrong. At the final studio screening of *Jaws* before we shipped the prints to all the theaters, I saw a way to make a cut that I hadn't been able to see the whole time.

Are public previews helpful to you?

FIELDS: I like to show it to audiences for an overall feeling of whether something works or not. It's amazing what happens in a preview: you cannot know for sure whether something hangs a little too long or is maybe a little too short.

When Spielberg was here, he mentioned a change you made after a preview—you found a little piece of film to extend the moment before the shark jumps out of the water at Roy Scheider.

FIELDS: Yeah, we tried to stall on it as long as we could. Somebody asked me the other day about the humor in *Jaws*; I think the humor is an enormous part of *Jaws* being a good picture. There were certain things we did not know were going to be big laughs. Nobody knew that Roy Scheider saying, after the shark jumps, "We need a bigger boat" was going to be an enormous laugh. As a matter of fact, we went back and looped it to try to raise the volume. Nobody ever hears that line thoroughly because they're still mumbling from the scream. I have tapes of the preview that are incredible because that audience not only went out of their seats, they carried on and talked for a full minute. And then in the middle of that came this line, "We need a bigger boat." The people who did hear it started screaming with laughter on top of the people talking and you couldn't hear a thing.

How does an editor work with the music cutter and the sound-effects cutter? How is the whole thing brought together?

FIELDS: Again, it depends. I'm a demon to work for because I was a sound cutter for years, but I think there is no one who knows the picture as well as the cutter, representing the director. Therefore if the director doesn't have time, the editor should sit down with the sound cutter and go over the picture very carefully. One can anticipate that a good sound editor knows that when a door closes you hear the door close. But what if you don't want to hear that door close for some reason? You really have to let them know what you want.

As far as the music is concerned, that needs to be worked on with the director; it's much less technical. But I did sit in on *Jaws*; [composer] John Williams, Steve, and I ran the picture and discussed and argued about where we thought music should start and where it should end. Everybody was receptive to everybody else's ideas. I would say that John's decisions were probably the prime ones. It was a good picture before it was scored, but his score did tremendous things for it. He and Steve played a lot of records; Steve had some very specific ideas about the kinds of music he wanted for the chases. John went off and wrote his music, and then we all went to a scoring session. Steve was there more than I was because we were pre-dubbing at that point. During the dubbing, I'll usually work without the director up to a point where I feel final decisions have to be made. Then I call in the director and we go for a take.

Do you have any theory about when and when not to cut to close-ups?

FIELDS: I have great admiration for a theory that Peter Bogdanovich has: he feels that it is an insult to an actor not to have done your homework well enough to know how you want the scene to play. What's this business of making a good actor do a good performance from six different angles? I think he has a very good point. In *Daisy Miller* [directed by Bogdanovich], we had a scene with fifty-four takes, trying to get perfection, but once he had that perfection, he did not ask them to do it again in a close-up or in a wider angle.

I looked at the dailies on another picture the other day and I could not believe what I was seeing. I saw the director do this, this, and this [gestures to indicate going from long shot to medium shot to close-up] on each person in the scene; then on two people in the scene; then on the whole scene; and then over the shoulders of everybody. On one scene which will probably cut to two and a half minutes, we saw an hour and twenty minutes' worth of dailies. I don't think the director had visualized the scene. Or his way of working is to shoot everything and then decide in the cutting room how he wants to play it. My favorite directors don't shoot that way.

Very often the director goes around saying, "The studio ruined my picture." Have you ever been involved in a situation like that, and whose side did you eventually feel closer to?

FIELDS: Fortunately, I never got into that kind of situation. It is true that there is a certain amount of cutting. When they make a deal with a director quite often they will have in the contract that he must deliver a film "no longer than . . ." and with a rating "no worse than . . . ," and if it doesn't, the studio has the right to take it into their own hands and do it. I don't think that's an unreasonable situation. There is a tendency on the part of a lot of directors to be self-indulgent, and I think the man putting up the money certainly has the right to try to protect his interest. A picture that's running overlong can't have as many showings in a theater.

The director knows this going in; he signed a contract agreeing to it; he has a certain responsibility to fulfill. I only know that I have seen studios being very, very reasonable on things like that. When a picture runs over the length, which it has in a couple cases [during Fields's tenure as a Universal executive], they have sat down and have tried to work with the director about it. I sound like I'm touting Universal, but I must say, now that I'm hearing what goes on from the other end, I'm amazed at how liberal they are with the filmmakers. They bend backward not to interfere, not to give them any trouble, and to give them all the support they can.

When you taught at USC, what do you think your students learned that might be useful to us?

FIELDS: The most useful thing I taught I can teach you all in about three minutes. In those days everybody had the feeling that all the old methods hampered them. When I remarked about coding the film and logging [methods of organizing the unedited footage and the outtakes], some young filmmakers said, "Cut by numbers like they do in the studios? I'm not cutting by numbers; I'm cutting by what's on the film." I was able to convince the students that in order to achieve real freedom in editing you have to be able to lay your hands on the exact piece of film you want when you want it. It's really dull, tedious, painful work, but you must log in and code your film. If you can't find that close-up, if it's in the bottom of the barrel somewhere, you have to cut to a second choice; you're really not free.

I think that was the main thing I told them. I can't say to you, "You've got to have rhythm." The mechanics are not hard to learn. But to get an impression across, or a story point, sometimes things that you thought would work just don't, and you realize you must do something to make it work.

You've mentioned that you shouldn't cover everything [shoot a scene from every possible angle]; are there things you would suggest to a director that he must do?

FIELDS: One should protect oneself with some coverage, because one of the problems with the way Peter Bogdanovich directs is that I may suddenly decide that a certain scene needs to be shortened, but I can't do it because he has not allotted the coverage. So, while I admire his theory [not shooting coverage], I think you should protect yourself because you do not always know when you shoot something that it's going to work. You particularly do not know if it's going to work when you see it with an audience.

Shooting a few extra feet of film might be the all-time savior. I see no reason in the world why a camera cuts off before a man exits, for example. And if you're doing an experimental or tricky move—like the terrific move that Steve did with the simultaneous zoom in and pull back on Roy Scheider during the shark attack at the beach—why have to go back another day if it doesn't work? Steve also shot a close-up of it even though he always intended to use this great shot.

How do you decide if a scene should play in a two-shot [a shot including two actors] without going into close-ups, or if a scene should play in a master?

FIELDS: I never cut away from a scene unless I feel it's not compelling me anymore or unless there's something else in the scene that I must see. But if I'm on a single [a shot including only one actor] or on a two-shot that is really telling me everything I need to know at that moment, why cut away from it?

You mentioned rhythm in cutting. What do you mean by that?

FIELDS: Let's see, how can I tell you? There's a feeling of movement in telling a story and there is a flow. A cut that is off-rhythm will be disturbing and you will feel it, unless you want it to be like that. On *Jaws,* each time I wanted to cut I didn't, so that it would have an anticipatory feeling—and it worked. A perfect example is the early beach scene; I broke the pace for the anticipation. You see a dog go into the water; you see a woman go into the water; you see someone else go into the water; and so forth. And the second time you see them you've now gotten the feeling that you expect a cut, and then all of a sudden I don't cut. I just hold it for about eight frames, in one case twelve frames [there are twenty-four frames per second of film], after I normally would have cut.

When you see *Taxi Driver* [directed by Martin Scorsese, edited by Sidney Levin], you're going to see a very good example of what can be done with editing. It is not cut in an ordinary smooth-flowing fashion; you are aware of cuts, and some are jarring, and they work incredibly well. That's the way the film is: it's shot rough. I don't mean jiggly—it's New York at its worst, it's grungy and it's a paranoid picture and it's irritating, and the editing helps create the feeling.

Cutting a film is really a matter of feeling. As far as I'm concerned, there are no rules except the film: the emotion or the impact of whatever you're trying to get. If it's a laugh you're trying to get or tears or a smile or a good feeling—whatever it is, if it works, do it.

THE COSTUME DESIGNER
Anthea Sylbert

For a costume designer to become a studio production executive is a most unusual transition, but Anthea Sylbert's costume design has always been an unusually important element in the overall impact of her films. Before she moved into the executive suite in 1977, she was much in demand for her fresh approach to costuming as an element of storytelling rather than mere decoration.

Sylbert received Academy Award nominations for her elegant but unobtrusive period designs for Roman Polanski's *Chinatown* (1974) and Fred Zinnemann's *Julia* (1977). She worked closely with her brother-in-law, production designer Richard Sylbert, on the vivid images of *Chinatown, Rosemary's Baby, Carnal Knowledge, The Fortune, The Heartbreak Kid,* and *Shampoo.* Her other notable films have included *A New Leaf, The Last Tycoon, King Kong,* and *F.I.S.T.*

Born in New York in 1939, she attended Barnard College and the Parsons School of Design. She worked for several years in the New York fashion industry (including a stint as a designer for Capezio shoes) and became involved in show business by designing clothes for friends in off-Broadway productions. In the mid-1960s she and her husband, director and production designer Paul

Sylbert (Richard's identical twin), relocated to Los Angeles, where she began designing costumes for films.

Her first film was *The Tiger Makes Out* (1967), followed by Polanski's influential horror film, *Rosemary's Baby*. Sylbert soon won the respect of other important directors with her ability to make costuming a vital and imaginative means of evoking character and subtly instilling time and place. Her work on the Warren Beatty/Robert Towne/Hal Ashby film *Shampoo*—a 1975 film set in a not-so-distant but very distinct 1968—was particularly striking as an inextricable ingredient in that film's commercial and critical success.

Sylbert was appointed vice-president for special projects by Warner Brothers in 1977, serving as liaison between filmmakers and the studio hierarchy. The following year she was promoted to production vice-president. While at Warners she was responsible for supervising the development of Paul Simon's *One Trick Pony* and Robert Towne's directorial debut, *Personal Best*.

Moving to United Artists in 1980 as production vice-president, she supervised such films as Barbra Streisand's directing debut, *Yentl*; Robert Benton's *Still of the Night*; and the contentious Don Siegel/Bette Midler collaboration, *Jinxed*. She left UA in 1982.

FILMOGRAPHY

1967 *The Tiger Makes Out*   1968 *Rosemary's Baby*   1969 *The Illustrated Man* / *Some Kind of a Nut* / *John and Mary*   1970 *Move*   1971 *A New Leaf* / *Carnal Knowledge*   1972 *The Cowboys* / *The Heartbreak Kid* / *Bad Company*   1973 *The Day of the Dolphin*   1974 *Chinatown*   1975 *Shampoo* / *The Fortune*   1976 *The Last Tycoon* / *King Kong*   1977 *Julia*   1978 *F.I.S.T.*

THE SEMINAR

Anthea Sylbert held a seminar with the Fellows of the Center for Advanced Film Studies on February 17, 1976.

One of the main aspects of costume design that would be of interest to everybody is how you begin your approach to the work when you read the screenplay.

SYLBERT: A costume designer really is an extension of the writer, the director, and the actor. If you do your job correctly and if you have done your thinking correctly, you have helped them; if not, you have sabotaged them. You start with a screenplay. You read it, and it gives you the settings; it gives you a year; it gives you the characters. Now, there are all sorts of decisions that have to be made about the characters if the information is not in the screenplay. What economic bracket are they in? What is their background? If they are rich, were they always rich? These are things that have to be decided with a director and, finally, an actor. To think that a costume designer just puts clothes on people is a mistake.

Let's take *Shampoo*. It is about a very specific place at a very specific time historically—Beverly Hills, California, on the day, night, and morning after the 1968 presidential election. It is almost more difficult when it is that close to you, because you start wanting to deny certain things that you did: "I didn't wear my skirts that short. I never could have done such a terrible thing." Then you start looking at photographs, and there it is: men did in fact open their shirts down to the navel and hang seven thousand things around their necks, started to become the peacocks, started in a funny way to become the sex object. Warren Beatty in that movie is the sex object. None of the women is. So you say, OK, if I'm going to put him in a leather jacket, I don't want a heavy leather jacket, I want it to be the softest leather jacket; when you touch it, it should almost be a sexual experience.

When I first did the sketch I made a mistake: I put zippers on the jacket. We started to make it, and I started to think that zippers are not really sexy, because they have something rigid about them and they are keeping me from seeing his body as well as I want to see it. We started from scratch again and we laced the jacket, had fringes hanging, so there was movement when he wore it. Even the jeans—we started off by just buying jeans; after all, jeans are jeans. Well, you couldn't see his body well enough, so we custom-made the jeans. His shirts were silk. Everything he wore had some kind of sexuality to it.

Now we have three females: we have a young girl, Goldie Hawn; we have a slightly older person, Julie Christie; then we have Lee Grant. Goldie Hawn is the epitome of the late '60s. It was one of the times when youth was revered and age was not. And whether you are going to custom-make her clothes or not, they must look like they cost $39.95 tops, because those girls had millions of clothes that fell apart in one day. Julie Christie, the Beverly Hills mistress, wears one of those silk blouses cut rather low, with a push-up bra, stuffed from underneath. This child [Goldie Hawn] wears no bra at all. There is only one scene where you see underwear in the movie, and that is where Lee Grant puts on a bra in the first sequence and Beatty says, "Take that off." Why would I concern myself with their underwear at all? Because it helps the actor to feel a certain thing, and whatever an actor is feeling should finally affect the audience. You give Julie Christie an uplifted bra with pads underneath and it makes her a whole other person; this lady probably buys her underwear at places like Frederick's of Hollywood. Not big on taste. She has a brain but she knows what it is she's using that brain for: it is to make herself most appealing to the men who are going to keep her.

Lee Grant has already gotten married. Who knows what she was before? We have to make certain decisions about her. I decided she probably was on the fringes of show business, probably had aspirations as an actress. Along came Jack Warden about twenty years ago; she married him before her budding career had blossomed, and there she is, this bored Beverly Hills housewife. She has nothing to do all day long but have her hair fixed and go shopping. And occasionally she has lunch with her girlfriends, and they all talk about their lovers. She does what they tell her to do in *Harper's Bazaar*. She has no style of her own. All she has is money. At that time one of the outfits *Harper's Bazaar* was pushing was a short skirt with thigh-high boots and a long fur coat. She's one of the few women in the film who wears fur during the day. It has nothing to do with weather: she's getting dressed for something else.

In other words, for a character like Lee Grant you have to take all the magazines from that time period, which then start to remind you of certain women you know. You start to think about what she did that was individual and peculiar in her choice of jewelry and accessories, little things that the audience may not see but will affect the performance. In her bag is every charge plate it is possible to possess; real live money hasn't a lot to do with her life. She probably has a few $100 bills that she uses only on rare occasions and some singles that are for parking boys. Those kinds of things are also part of a costume designer's obligation to that actress. Your obligation is to help the director and the actor create an atmosphere and an attitude, and your obligation does not end with what you can physically see: it has to do with giving the actor underwear, keys, stuffing pockets, having the actor wear the clothes, get used to them. If it can be afforded, it is a good thing to give a woman like that real jewelry—not that it photographs any differently, but it makes her feel different.

Should an actor wear his costumes and get used to them before shooting?

SYLBERT: You must make them early enough for the actors to wear them. Except for gowns, let's say, that are going to be worn as if they're brand-new, practically all other costumes should be worn by actors and should be ready by rehearsal time, which on a movie of any size is usually at least a two-week period. I just finished doing some clothes for Jack Nicholson in *The Last Tycoon*. We sent the suit by special messenger to New York, where he was, and the instructions were, "Do not take it off. The most important thing you must do is travel on the plane in it, which is what the character would have done." Being the good actor that he is, he did that.

When you make decisions about characterization, do you make them with the actors and the director all in a group?

SYLBERT: It depends on the personality of the director how involved he becomes. Some directors say, "OK, go ahead." In a funny way it is easier to work with a director who is to a certain extent dictatorial, as long as he's not completely interfering. I like to think of them as benevolent dictators. When you are aware of what style they intend to use photographically, what colors they wish to avoid, what painter they might wish to approximate, it makes your job much easier. When a director is vague, you are doing part of his job by making those choices for him.

Someone like Mike Nichols will usually have a painter in mind, or he might have a kind of photography in mind. In *The Fortune* it was the look of advertising photography during the 1920s that gave the color key. It was very apricot and beige, white, rusty and red. It was a very romantic palette—perhaps not an appropriate palette to the material, but it was a choice. Any choice is better than no choice at all.

Certain actors also become more involved than others. I like actors to become involved only in character decisions. If Lee Grant had decided "No, she had always had money; in fact, it was *her* money that helped *him* to begin with," then I would have made certain changes. But once having gone along with the choice that *"I'm* the one who in fact had no money; perhaps he had a little bit of money when we started, and I probably worked along with him to help him get some of it, which is why I think it is my due to have as much as possible"—then I get slightly dictatorial about how that is expressed, only because I have more time to give thought to that. And unless I have gone completely astray, actors usually will accept my decisions, because they understand when you have done something that has helped their character. If a good actor starts to reject it, I listen; it may very well be an indication that I have gone wrong. I have very rarely been in a situation where some kind of compromise is not possible. Sometimes, however, you believe so strongly in what you have done that you will fight for it.

Sometimes the writer will put a description of the costumes in the script. Do you go by that?
SYLBERT: Only if he's a very good writer. I don't understand it when a writer says, "She was sitting in the audience in a pink dress." I say to him, "Do you have a reason why she's wearing a pink dress?" He usually doesn't. A writer very often can't see— that's why he writes—unless he's a wonderful writer who has a good eye. For instance, Joseph Conrad had a very good eye; if we were making *Victory* tomorrow I would pay very close attention

to what he said about the clothes, because they were not arbitrary choices. They were very specific choices which had to do with giving the atmosphere and the background of that person. When he describes a "white lawn dress with that strange red ribbon that goes across it," he is not being arbitrary; he is making tacky at the same time that he is making pretty, and he's making vulnerable; he's making all those things. Then I'd listen.

Do you work closely with the hairdresser?

SYLBERT: Very. Sometimes successfully now. Usually the hairdresser comes on late, so the clothes are done already. Hairdressers are funny people. In the theater a hairdresser would never think about starting on a hairdo without consulting the costume designer. Here, if you say, "What kind of hairdo is that?" they go to somebody and say, "She is in violation [of craft jurisdictional rules]." Technically, you *are* in violation. Touching hair is out of the question altogether. All you want to do is muss it a bit, because if you could get your fingers through it for a minute you know you could make the actor look like a person. So it depends on putting together a crew which is flexible and cooperative enough to work together without all those silly rules that have nothing to do with filmmaking. After all, it is a cooperative venture, and we are all working on one movie.

Are you always on the set during the making of a movie?

SYLBERT: You don't just design something and say goodbye. What if I get an idea at the last minute and want to change something? The more prepared you are, the more flexible it can become for you, because then you can be free enough to take advantage of the accidents that occur. If you are muddled with trying to keep up, you cannot take advantage of the accidents; you are in no state of mind to recognize the accident when it happens, much less take advantage of it. I may look at something and all of a sudden say, "It would be better if she were wearing a red rose." That might make a scene. Or the purse I have given an actress makes it impossible for her to do her activity. A wardrobe person would sit there and say, "I'm terribly sorry, but the designer said this is the purse that goes with this outfit, and you have to carry it." It's crazy.

The other reason I like to stay on the set is that I think the more you understand everybody's problem and how everybody does his work, the more you can do yours well, and the more yours will be a service to the film.

When you're doing a scene, say in Goldie Hawn's apartment, do you think there would be an advantage in letting the production designer prepare the room and you the costumes, and then bringing it all together to see what happens?

SYLBERT: It's better to plan. It's better for me to know what colors he's going to be using, what attitude he's taking toward her apartment. If you're going to make it an apartment of a girl who seems to have some kind of family allowance, which I think that apartment was, then you know something about her physical surroundings which should help you in clothes. You could also decide that she has spent nothing on her apartment and wears every penny on her back. But that also is a decision that should be made up front; it's leaving too much to chance to let the production designer or art director, the set decorator, and the costume designer stay in three separate worlds doing whatever it is they do and then come together. What if it doesn't spell "Mother"? It's almost too late to fix it.

Do you feel that most people dress to fit their character or are they dressing to fit something else?

SYLBERT: Well, even then they're telling you something about themselves. Even when people decide to look like they don't care about clothes, there is a certain way of putting it together that says one kind of "I don't care" and another that says a different kind. When you dress actors against the character, you are saying something about them, and that's another thing you must consider. An extremely wealthy person who insists on wearing glasses that are taped and an old pair of baggy khakis and a tweed jacket that has its seventh set of leather patches on the elbows and a shirt that maybe has a hole in it—you know all sorts of things about this person, especially if he steps out of a Rolls Royce.

When we make pictures here our budgets are counted in dollars rather than millions. How do you cut corners without sacrificing quality?

SYLBERT: You have to steal. All of the extras' clothing in *Shampoo* was borrowed from friends. I didn't do it because we didn't have the money to do costumes; I did it because I didn't know any other way to do it. I can go and buy thirty or forty dresses from the '20s or '30s or '40s, but I could not find one from the '60s. So you go to the telephone and say, "Hello, what do you have left over in your closet from around 1968?" At first they're a little hesitant, but you have to keep conning them until in fact you get somebody to give you a Galanos.

On your first film you're probably not going to have a lot of money. That is the time when the most thinking has to occur, and the most eliminating. I can make a period bedroom—and I have seen it done—with one perfect bedstead and a wonderful lamp. You don't need a lot of other things. If a character reads like she should have fifteen costume changes, make do with four, but have those four be really perfect for the character and let them repeat as in life. Everyone I know, even the richest person, repeats clothing, except for one very insane woman I know. So unless the character in this movie is insane there is no reason why every time you see her she is wearing something different.

If a producer came to you and you presented him with these sketches from Shampoo *for the leads, would you make an estimate of how much it would cost?*

SYLBERT: Yes. I know that to make a gown like this one for Julie Christie in the scene at the Bistro will cost about $1,200. If I went out to buy a real Galanos or a real Norell, it would cost more like $3,000, so I say it's a bargain that we have here. If you say to me, "I can't afford that," then my answer is, "Let's make a movie about poor people."

Would you make only one of those dresses?

SYLBERT: That's the next decision we have to make. She is going to walk around with these crazies who could very well spill a glass of red wine all over her. Do we want to take the chance of doing that, or do we want to spend another $1,200 and have two? I would say, "You tell me. After all, I could probably whip one up in about a day and a half while you're all sitting there waiting, or maybe you could be shooting something else." A shooting day could cost $25,000. So what do we think? I suspect we make two.

Are there some films that don't need a costumer?

SYLBERT: Certain filmmakers assume that if you're doing a modern film nobody has to sit down and make a sketch and then make a costume. In the theater it would never occur to anybody producing a play—no matter where or when it took place or how many characters it had—to start without a costume designer. A costume designer is always valuable to a director and an actor. And the costume part of a budget is usually the smallest part of a budget.

The hardest kind of movie to costume is a completely modern movie. Everybody is an expert because everybody wears clothes, and everybody has an opinion. It's usually wrong and you don't want to hear it, but you have to go through that process.

The other difficult thing about doing a movie that takes place "today" is that it's really going to take place a year later. If somebody in the movie was trying to be very "with it," I would try to figure out what would be "with it" by the time the movie opened, try to anticipate what might happen in the fashion world, which is not necessarily easy. Things can change even within a year. Let's say today is 1948 and last year was 1947: the change would be quite large, because all of a sudden hemlines have dropped, waists have gone in.

When we did *Rosemary's Baby*, in 1968, Roman Polanski insisted on setting it in the year the Pope visited the United States—1965. That year was also the beginning of the shortening of skirts. I remember in my own life being rather timid about all this, once a month taking up a half-inch and then another half-inch and another—we started out below the knee and ended up about mid-thigh. It never got to be the real miniskirt, but during the progression of the movie, subtle though it may be, Rosemary's skirts go up. There's a scene where she's sewing one.

In a period film do you try to use the genuine fabric of the time?
SYLBERT: Even today one can find a real piece of wool or a piece of satin if one is willing to look for it. It is not necessary to use polyester; in fact, it is out of the question to use it. In *Chinatown* there is not a piece of polyester. Some designers don't think that way. I think authenticity is necessary not only for how the clothing falls, but also for how the person feels in it. If I put a real piece of silk on a girl, she is going to feel different from the way she feels if I give her some polyester shit.

In *The Last Tycoon*, Theresa Russell, who plays the daughter of the head of the studio, had never acted in a film before. She is supposed to be quite wealthy, and they attempted to buy things off the rack and then vaguely alter them to look like period. They had this idea that they were going to "insinuate" the period. Whatever that means I don't want to know. I think it came out of the idea that they did not want the period to take over.

The period should *never* take over. This is a rule I think you should use when you're working on a period film. Let's say we're all going to start work on a movie that takes place in 1927: I think we suspend the thought that it is 1976; it *is* 1927. It actually *is*. Once it is, it is not necessary to do things like inserts of clutches, because that's the way cars come; they don't come any other way, so it is not odd. Everything about the period becomes natural.

Anyway, they bought a lot of polyester and stuck it on Theresa Russell. She looked terrible. I got a call from the producer, Sam Spiegel, and I met Theresa. I said, "First of all, she's supposed to be rich, so give her something luxurious. Make her *look* luxurious so she can perhaps even begin to feel rich about herself." For the first scene I decided to pretend that she had just come from golf. Let's establish someone who is more athletic than graceful. So her first outfit became this golfing outfit, all real wool and thin handkerchief linen for the blouse. It did not affect her that much yet, but she could tell something was going on. The second outfit was a simple blouse and a skirt, but the blouse was silk, the skirt was really wool, the stockings were silk, her shoes were wonderful. Theresa, who is only eighteen or nineteen, puts this outfit on, and now we're trying to pin and she's doing this [stroking the clothing]. I allowed her to do it for a little while, but finally I said,"Now, stop. We must get to work here." Even an inexperienced actress starts to move another way when she feels the things you have put on her.

Do you always rely on photographs for historical research?
SYLBERT: Absolutely. I always use photographs of people who exist, even for fictional characters. Surely if one is doing a historical story one is obligated to research it to a certain extent. You might decide, however, that you could come up with something that would work better dramatically. But you can only make that decision after you have discovered what the reality is. I have hardly had an original idea in my entire life. I only take them from real people in real photographs, very rarely even from fashion magazines, because they are misleading.

It also depends on the kind of film you are doing. If it's about the Civil War, there are several American painters you should look at. They give you clues about coloring. I worked on a small movie called *Bad Company*, and instead of making historically accurate Union uniforms, the color was changed to be as it was painted. After all, you are to a certain extent painting when you make a movie.

If you're doing a comedy set in the 1920s, then you look at [magazine illustrator John] Held. If you know anybody who was alive at that time or who has a relative who was alive, that's the first person you go to. You say, "Listen, is there any way Aunt Sarah would allow me to have her album of photographs from when she was nineteen in 1928?" That's always the best form of research: snapshots. And when you're walking through flea markets or whatever and see something that has nothing to do with what you're working on now but seems interesting, buy it, label it, and put it away. *The American Album* [a 1968 book of historical photographs compiled by the editors of *American Heritage* magazine], for instance, has wonderful photographs. In the back are the credits of the photographers; then you can look for their books, and you slowly accumulate your own research library. You go through a newspaper and see a particularly wonderful photograph of people at a convention. Tear it out, because you will not be able to remember it. You may never use it, but what does it hurt to tear it out and put it in this little envelope that says, "1974— U.S. types, political"?

Is there a tendency to design not only for the period of the film but also for today?

SYLBERT: Well, to some extent you may make certain alterations to make a modern audience feel more comfortable. If we were doing a movie set in the 1940s, we would want only to suggest wide shoulders rather than making everybody look like they are playing dress-up. Some actors can carry clothes better than others. When they cannot, it is better to cheat the period a little.

But one must never design with the thought of impressing the fashion world. I think it's the worst thing you can do, because then the movie becomes about the costumes. It must never be about the costumes; it must always be about the characters. You must not leave a movie whistling the clothes.

THE AGENT
Sue Mengers

In today's Hollywood there is no one more powerful than the agent, and Sue Mengers is perhaps the most powerful agent in town. Her roster of star actors and directors reads like a *Who's Who* of bankable names, and her deal-making prowess has been celebrated in the popular press.

Among Mengers's clients at International Creative Management (ICM) have been Barbra Streisand, Faye Dunaway, Mike Nichols, Peter Bogdanovich, Ryan and Tatum O'Neal, Gene Hackman, Sidney Lumet, Arthur Penn, Michael Caine, George Segal, Ali MacGraw, and Joan Micklin Silver. Mengers has negotiated on their behalf some of the most lucrative deals ever made in Hollywood, while shrewdly building their careers as artists.

Mengers herself reached "star" status in the early 1970s, when several magazine profiles portrayed her as a brassy, flamboyant, hard-as-nails Hollywood character; she later said she "resented the fact that the press, in order to write about a lady agent, had to make me into a caricature." Along the same lines, she served as the model for the agents played on screen by Dyan Cannon in *The Last of Sheila* and by Shelley Winters in Blake Edwards's *S.O.B.*

The power Mengers wields is reflective of the changes the

film industry has undergone since World War II. With the break-down of the studio system and the demise of long-term contracts, agents stepped into the power void and today are more often responsible than studio executives for initiating and packaging film projects. Indeed, it has become a natural progression for agents to become heads of studios. ICM, the agency through which Mengers works, is the largest in the business.

"I never grew up wanting to be an agent," she has said. "I grew up wanting to marry and have children." Born in Germany in the mid-1930s, she left with her parents in 1939 and settled in the Bronx. She started her career as a receptionist and secretary for MCA, then a theatrical agency. Although she found secretarial training useful, she also found it limiting, and left MCA for Baum-Newborn, a hustling freelance agency.

From there she went into an apprenticeship with the William Morris Agency, and in 1963 formed a partnership with Tom Korman, one of her colleagues at Baum-Newborn. In the mid-1960s, David Begelman, then a partner in Creative Management Associates, brought her to Hollywood; CMA merged with Marvin Josephson Associates to form ICM in 1975. Since then Mengers has remained firmly ensconced in her power base within ICM, resisting frequent offers of studio executive positions.

THE SEMINAR

Sue Mengers held a seminar with the Fellows of the Center for Advanced Film Studies on March 5, 1976.

What do you look for when you take on a client?
MENGERS: Money. The potential to earn money. At the moment, because a lot of the clients I took on when they were unknowns have become knowns, I am not interested in taking on new clients unless some of my other clients leave. But I started out, for instance, representing Peter Bogdanovich after seeing *Targets*. I didn't get him *The Last Picture Show*, but he had just gotten the assignment and no one was that impressed that he had an under-$1-million feature to direct. I was very fortunate that his career accelerated. But when I did start representing him he was an unknown. Ryan O'Neal was also an unknown; *Love Story* had not yet opened when I started representing Ryan. Gene Hackman is another one. I started representing him when he was a featured player, and again we got fortunate with *The French Connection*.

I guess it's instinct and luck. And also, when you represent one well-known person, somehow that makes other well-known people feel secure. They figure, "If she's got Barbra Streisand she must be OK."
On What's Up, Doc? *you had Barbra Streisand, Ryan O'Neal, and Peter Bogdanovich, so I presume that you presented a package to the studio.*
MENGERS: Actually, I didn't. The term "package" is the most misused term in our industry. Very seldom is there such a thing as a package. It sometimes happens that an agent represents all the people involved, but if you represent a director you can't say, "Hey, take these two stars because they happen to be my clients." If it happens to work that way, great, but that's more a coincidence than a package. *What's Up, Doc?* started out as a project for Streisand. With Barbra's approval we—[Warner Brothers executive] John Calley and I—then brought in Bogdanovich, who then agreed to use Ryan O'Neal. So it just evolved that way.

As for the actual mechanics of negotiation, first and foremost is always salary. Then billing. Usually stars' contracts are pretty standard; a lawyer comes in and does the more detailed work.

What does an agent need from a director to sell the person?

MENGERS: Well, I must be honest. I doubt if I could have sold Bogdanovich for *What's Up, Doc?* based on *Targets*. He got *Last Picture Show* based on his relationship with producer Bert Schneider, and it's a credit to Streisand, Calley, and Ryan that they looked at a rough cut of *Last Picture Show* and recognized his talent.

I think for a first-time director the answer is good material for the lowest-possible budget. The superstars who can get projects going are leery of first-time directors, and only if they feel the material is something they would die if they didn't do will they give someone a shot. That's a generalization, you know, and there have been instances—Charlie Bronson and Walter Hill [Hill made his directing debut on Bronson's *Hard Times*, which he also wrote]—so again it depends. A screenwriter who has done three or four valid screenplays and then writes an original that's good—yes, I think a star might be more inclined to take a shot. But it's tough.

I'm curious about whether you find that the people in the industry have enough faith in themselves when they read a property to say "I know this is good" or "I know this is bad"?

MENGERS: Today the studios are generally less adventurous than ever before, because the few films they are doing are costing so much. I'm a very negative person and I always think nothing good is going to happen, but every once in a while it does. Joan Silver's husband [Rafael Silver] had absolutely no connections in the business; he just went out and raised $400,000 or $500,000 and she did *Hester Street*. And as a result of that, today if there were a property around, Joan Silver would have a shot at directing it as well as anyone else.

How did you come to take her on as a client?

MENGERS: I read a review that Charles Champlin wrote in the *Los Angeles Times* on *Hester Street* while it was still at the Cannes Film Festival, before it opened here or had a distributor. I liked what I read in the review, and I called her and arranged to see the film. I liked the film and told her I'd like to see if I could help her sell it to a distributor. I was not successful, and her husband ended up distributing it himself, very successfully. But I was very impressed with her. An agent's dream is a writer-director, because that's someone who can create her own material and is not sitting there saying "Get me a job." She didn't say to me, "Can I do Barbra Streisand's next picture?" She said, "Listen, I've got a couple of ideas for scripts I want to write." I like the ideas she is developing, and I hope I'll be able to help her set them up. [Silver later directed *Between the Lines*, 1977, and *Head Over Heels/Chilly Scenes of Winter*, 1979.]

Do you think the industry is opening up for women to become directors?

MENGERS: Yes, I think so. I don't think women are going to have an easier time than men. It depends on their validity. If Lee Grant had a piece of material that someone wanted to do very badly, they'd give her a shot because of Lee's experience as an actress. [Grant made her feature directing debut with *Tell Me a Riddle*, 1980.] I don't think an unknown woman has any better chance than an unknown man. I think it's equal.

It's as hard to get work today for superstars and superstar directors as it is for anyone else. Everyone is suffering from the depressed industry. I get furious when I read articles about how much money everyone is making. Well, a very few are making a lot of money, but there isn't enough work to sustain an entire industry today, because if a studio does two $12-million movies that's their budget for the year. That may give a lot of money to the people involved in those two movies, but what about the other people? I've got a lot of clients—major names—who don't have their next pictures.

What responsibility do agents have in this trend toward huge productions?

MENGERS: I really blame the studios. I can't say to a star client of mine that he should take less than a rival star client. No one is forcing the studios to pay these prices. And as long as they're dumb enough—I mean, Gene Hackman did not want to do *Lucky Lady*. They kept offering him more and more and more money. Well, everyone has his price. It wasn't as though he was being asked to exterminate people: he was being asked to play in a movie. And finally 20th Century-Fox came up with so much money [$1.25 million] that it was almost obscene for him *not* to do the film.

Now, why? With all due respect to Gene Hackman, they couldn't have believed it was going to make that much difference at the box office. And the minute they paid that money, Jack Nicholson said, "Wait a minute. If Gene Hackman gets that much money I should get X." And Warren Beatty says, "Well, if Nicholson gets that, I should get X." And it became crazed. I don't think it was *my* fault.

Do you always negotiate the points [percentage points of net profit or gross] in the picture as well?

MENGERS: It depends on the strength of the client. When you don't get participation, your front money naturally accelerates. It's usually one or the other. Very few stars can command enormous participation, like gross from the first dollar. The best participation is if you can get gross from every box-office dollar. The next best is gross after break-even, which means when the picture has paid back its negative cost and its advertising. After that, profits. But [producer] Joe Levine, who is getting criticized for the prices he is paying on *A Bridge Too Far*, also is not giving participation. So if you're a Robert Redford, you may get $2 million for doing it, but what if suddenly the picture turns out to be *Jaws* [at that time the top money-making film in history]? Had you had your normal deal, which in Redford's case would be gross from the first dollar, he could have walked away from it with untold sums of money. So producers have to make that choice: if they don't want to give up participation, they have to give more front money.

I've always been amazed that the studios never seem to take a balanced or portfolio approach to the financing of films: a few small-budget films, a few medium-budget films, and a few large-budget films. They all seem to want to do the best and biggest. Is there a reason for that? Is that ego coming into play?

MENGERS: You've got to remember that the people in the studios are salaried employees. They are not owners. They are people who are employed by boards of directors, and they're scared. When you're dealing out of insecurity it's hard to make good creative decisions. Those jobs should only belong to rich people; when you were Louis B. Mayer [head of MGM from the 1920s through 1951], making a fortune because of the tax structure in those days, plus having ownership, you were able to go more with your instincts.

It's like the agents who have their own agencies and are totally dependent upon their clients for the commission—sometimes you might find yourself recommending something to a client because you want that client to go to work so you can make some money. If you're with a large agency, have a contract, and know you're going to get paid whether your client works that year or not, you're able to be much more objective about what a client should or shouldn't do.

Do you have any desire to produce?

MENGERS: Not at all. That's the last thing I would do. I would imagine that to do it well you really have to spend a long time nurturing something and developing it, and I don't have the temperament for that. I need much more varied activity.

Is there a dearth of good material?

MENGERS: Yes, there always is. And it's also a question of "Who knows what's good?" I mean, I know what's bad, but I don't know what's good. I have read very little lately that I liked or could get excited about, and I don't know what the answer is. I think the answer is that a lot of young writers can't afford to write. They just can't afford the luxury of sitting down and writing. I keep trying to talk to the producers: "Subsidize some of the young writers. Give them some money so they can write originals." Because that's really where it comes from.

Writers are the lowest men on the totem pole. I'm married to one [Jean-Claude Tramont], so I'm very passionate about the subject. Writers are treated very badly by directors. Again, this is a real generalization, but I find that the egos of most directors are such that if they commit to a screenplay, which they obviously liked well enough to commit to, then they immediately have to change it totally so they can justify that it's really theirs. A big ego trip. I must say I resent that. I've seen material that actors and actresses commit to, and then the day of shooting it's a whole new script because suddenly the director has to become the auteur. It's terribly unfair.

The other problem about the material is that a lot of the stars work less now because they are making so much money. If you get $1 million a picture, your motivation to do three a year is not that strong. When the front money was $350,000 tops, an actor, even a star, would do two or three pictures a year. Now they're so rich that the material has to be really stimulating, especially for them to go off on location.

How much advice do you give your clients about which projects to do?

MENGERS: It depends on the individual. I like to think that my opinions matter. With some clients they matter more than with others. Bogdanovich couldn't care less what I think about the material he picks. Neither could Mike Nichols or Sidney Lumet, whom I told not to do *Murder on the Orient Express*—none of my director clients really cares that much about my opinion about material. They decide what they want to do and they just want my help in getting them that project or setting up that project. The actors and actresses I represent are more interested in what I think. Directors really have to be much more secure in what they want to do. I don't pretend to know that much.

Have you taken any of your clients from the area of feature films and suggested they do television?

MENGERS: I'm a great believer in television, but I don't think there's any reason for Peter Bogdanovich to do television today. I don't think television has grown with him. Television is a terrific place for newcomers. I was heartsick when the Movies of the Week were discontinued; that was such a terrific place for young writers and producers and directors to get started. For actresses I strongly recommend television because there's so little work in films. Susan Clark and Elizabeth Montgomery have better roles on their television specials than most of our female stars play in films. Same thing with actors. I still say Jimmy Caan became a star out of *Brian's Song* [a 1972 TV movie], not *The Godfather*. He argues it with me, but I disagree.

What are the differences between a small agency and a large agency?

MENGERS: There are advantages and disadvantages. The problem with a small agency, unfortunately, is that there isn't as much coverage of what's going around. At one time I thought of opening my own agency, and then I thought, "Well, if I'm at Warner Brothers, then I can't be at Fox." At a large agency, with all the impersonality that's attributed to it, at least you get the benefit of all the input of the one hundred agents or whatever. But in any kind of agent-client relationship, you're never with an agency, you're with an agent. And if you find an agent with whom you have a rapport, who believes in you, you should follow that agent whether that agent goes to a big agency or a small agency.

What percentage of agents are women?

MENGERS: Well, I'm from New York, and most of the New York theater and literary agents are women. I don't know why that is. I guess because they've always worn hats, and hats seem to have a literary image. There are starting to be a few more women motion-picture agents. It's slowly happening, but like the rest of the business, there aren't very many openings right now for new agents because there isn't that much employment. A lot of the big agencies used to take their agents from the mailroom, and most girls never became mailroom boys. You can't just become an agent; it takes years and years of contacts. A producer could become an agent. My own background was from the secretarial route.

Did you feel any substantial change in how the industry viewed you once you became a married woman?

MENGERS: I was taken more seriously after I got married. When you're dealing in as competitive a business as the agency business, and you're dealing on the level that I wanted to be involved on, the high-money level, everything counts: where you live, whom you're married to, you're totally judged. The people you represent are so insecure. If they know that you're a nice married lady and not out getting stoned at a discothèque, somehow it does make them feel more secure. That's one of the reasons I'm trying to stop the publicity that helped me in the beginning; someone said, "How would you like to read about your business manager in *Cosmo?*" People don't want a character representing them; they want someone with an eyeshade who they think sits and reads scripts all night.

I'm not really a feminist, but I must say that I resented the fact that, in order to write about a lady agent, the press had to make me into a caricature. It didn't occur to them that a woman in this business could be successful just because she was smart and worked hard. I'm very angry about it. Even though it helped me in a strange way, I want to withdraw from it now because I think it could hurt me.

Could you explain how an agent covers a studio?

MENGERS: What you try to do at least once a month is get brought up to date by the head of the studio, the head of production, about their schedule: "What films have you bought? What books have you bought?" Then you try to sell them writers for the books, and you try to sell them directors or actors. Each studio has producers who work on the lot, so you also go and visit them and find out at what stage their projects are. The most vital thing an agent can contribute to her clients is to know what's going on at the studios and what's available. The most horrible thing for me would be for a client to miss a job because I didn't know about it.

Do the studios and the producers encourage agents to visit them on the lot?

MENGERS: Right now agents have more power than the studios. Studios need the agents because the agents are the major suppliers of talent and material. What used to drive us crazy is that we would work very hard to help put a picture together and then the picture would be finished, there would be a preview, and we would be told that no agents were allowed. You know, like those signs, "No soliciting, no agents." And only recently has that stopped because some of us said, "The hell with you. How dare you? We made as much of a contribution to this film as this studio did." Slowly now the image of the agent is returning to one of much more importance, much more respect.

Do you believe people really go to see the stars?

MENGERS: That's something we could debate. Sometimes they do, sometimes they don't. We could give fifty examples. They go to see Warren Beatty in *Shampoo*; they don't go to see Warren Beatty in *The Fortune*. They go to see Streisand in *The Way We Were*; they don't go to see Streisand in *Up the Sandbox*. The theory of the studios—and I'm not sure I agree with them—is that if you have a successful film, having a star in it adds to the success of that film; if it's not a successful film, the star equalizes it. Take, for instance, *The Towering Inferno*. I kept saying, "Why do they need McQueen and Newman in *Towering Inferno*?" They claim they got more gross, and that even though it would have been a huge picture without McQueen and Newman, it was an even bigger picture with McQueen and Newman. And I guess I have to agree with them, if they've got the figures. Also, the studios are very oriented toward getting money out of the overseas market, and certain names mean a great deal. McQueen is worth his weight in gold in Europe and Japan. When we read about the money McQueen is offered, we think it is shocking, but if Japan says to a studio, "Look, we'll give you $5 million just based on your getting McQueen," then maybe McQueen is worth the money, because they get it up front.

In the case of an actor like McQueen who is constantly being asked to work rather than looking for work, is the agent earning his or her commission, and if so, how?

MENGERS: I sometimes ask myself that. I really do. I have to believe that we do something. I have to believe that there's some reason Barbra Streisand pays me 10 percent. I don't have to sit awake nights wondering what she's going to do next. But I have to believe that I help guide her; I have to believe I keep a lot of material away from her that I know isn't in her area of interest. You see, a star pays for the privilege of privacy. A McQueen couldn't possibly talk to every producer, writer, director who wants to work with him. Therefore, he wants to have one person who is close to him professionally and privy to what he is interested in and whom he wants to work with. Maybe you think it's a lot of money to pay for that little information, but actors pay for the privilege of your being their intermediary with the world. You cannot imagine the pressures on the superstars. They need not just someone to fluff them, but someone to say, "Hey, Barbra, you should take this meeting" or "Hey, McQueen, you should read this script." And I guess most of us are doing something right because they are still with us.

In most cases, do they leave before you tell them to?

MENGERS: It's usually mutual. I've been an agent for twelve years now, and I've lost very few clients. I was only surprised once by someone leaving me, and I felt that was unjustified and I got that client back. I can almost predict when I start to represent someone whether it's going to last, because I'm very dominant, you know, and I have to like the people I work with. Now, in some cases I've held on because they were worthwhile professionally. But ultimately you cannot have a long, lasting relationship with a client you don't like. It's impossible.

Do you have any advice for a young actor or actress scouting around for an agent?

MENGERS: Oh, I'm the wrong one to ask because I'm so cynical about it. Everyone wants to be an actor or actress, you know; *I* would love to be a movie star. I don't know what the answer is. I think casting people are better for that today than agents are. Agents have to earn their salary, and today even the small agencies can't take on unknowns. There are a lot of really good casting directors who are constantly looking for new faces to fill up the television shows. There's a new star who's just been made out of *Rich Man, Poor Man*—Nick Nolte. Nick Nolte is now hot. I mean, Nick Nolte is being offered major leads in films. And how did he get that job? He met a casting director who sent him up, he was seen with twenty other guys, he did readings, he went that route, and as a result of it he did get an agent. Casting directors have open doors: they'll see everybody and they'll remember faces and they'll do auditions, because that's their job.

I wonder if you sometimes consider yourself almost a surrogate mother, especially to actors—

MENGERS: Do I seem maternal to you?

—and if you ever find yourself getting too involved in someone's problems?

MENGERS: It depends. There are one or two clients I'm close to because it's just been so many years that we've been together. But the other day I was a little depressed, and I thought, even though there are clients who are really close friends, there is still that barrier because you can't expose yourself too much, your weaknesses, because you're still the person involved in their business. It's unfortunate, but I feel they really do not want to know. I would not be thrilled if my business manager called up and said, "I'm depressed." "What do you mean, depressed? What's happening to my money?" Some of my clients are much closer to me than I am to them, let's put it that way. If I were really sick I think they would be concerned, but on the level of "What will happen to me?" I don't think it's selfish, necessarily. It's just that it is a very vulnerable area when you're dealing with someone's career.

You said that when you take on clients you measure their earning potential. I assume you're talking about people who already have significant credits. How do you measure the potential of someone who doesn't have any credits? Would you consider developing the career of that kind of person?

MENGERS: Not right now, because I have a responsibility to be loyal to the people who gave me my opportunity. I can't say to them, "Because you're successful you don't need me." Stars need advice and help as much as beginners do.

I'm not some genius who can sit in a room with an aspiring director and hear him talk and know whether he can do it. I just know that the Steve Spielbergs, the Martin Scorseses, the Joan Silvers somehow went out and did it. They didn't have agents at the time; they just did it. The AFI does give you some opportunity to have your work seen. I don't know how else to do it.

Short Subjects

NICHOLAS RAY, director

"You can't teach film. I don't give a goddamn who says it, *you can't teach film*."

FRITZ LANG, director

"I like audiences. I was always opposed to the American line, 'An audience has the mentality of a sixteen-year-old chambermaid.' If this were true, I would be ashamed to work for such an audience. I don't think you should give an audience something fifty steps ahead of them. Why is the first work of a writer, a screenwriter, or a playwright almost always a success? Because he still belongs to an audience. The more he goes away from the audience, the more he loses contact. What I tried to do my whole life long was not to lose contact with the audience."

FRANK CAPRA, director

"I think of the medium as a people-to-people medium—not cameramen to people, not directors to people, not writers to people, but people to people. You can only involve an audience with people. You can't involve them with gimmicks, with sunsets, with hand-held cameras, with zoom shots, or anything else. They couldn't care less about those things; but you give them some person they can worry about and care about, and you've got them involved. Everything is subject to the actors, as far as I'm concerned. I try to make the actor live the part and not act it, because my main objective is to get the audience to believe what they're seeing up there on the screen and become part of it. If I can involve the audience that much, then that's remarkable.

179

"Nobody has ever had the power a filmmaker has. No saint, no pope, no general, no sultan has ever had the power a filmmaker has: the power to talk to hundreds of millions of people for two hours in the dark. You have this power as filmmakers. You have the power to say anything you want, so why not say something positive?"

ALEXANDER MACKENDRICK, director and teacher

"One of the compliments I treasure was paid to me many years ago. An aunt of mine who lived near the Ealing Studios [in England] had her flat redecorated by a painter. It turned out that he was working on and off at the studio as a standby painter. He said to my aunt, 'Mackendrick? Any relation to the guy who is working over at Ealing?' She said yes. And he said, 'Oh, that's great. He worked on several of my films.' I think that's a compliment to me, because if I am a good director I hope that what I do is make everybody assume that it's his film.

"The nature of the filmmaking process, from the origin of an idea to the last moment when the damned thing is mixed and dubbed and shown in the theater, is one process. The fact that the process passes from person to person and that each of them should think he did the whole thing is how it should be. If there is one interpretation it's wrong. I am nothing but the centripetal force that holds these interpretations together. I may privately think I did it all, but if I do I'm kidding myself, because I am the channel of other people's talents."

HASKELL WEXLER, cinematographer

"Film is an artistic, human expression, and as such, people, particularly students, should give serious thought to what they want to express—what their art is, what their ideas are about life, about people, about humanity, about why we're here and what we're doing. But if you want to be comfortable, if you think a lot about lenses, F-stops, zoom ranges, and two-frame pulldowns or full-frame 35 or Techniscope, you can get quite involved with that and forget what it's all about.

"I would suggest that a great deal of thought and conversation with one another as artists and as filmmakers should go into thinking about why you are making films, what kinds of films you want to make, why you want to make those films. What I notice about many of my friends or people who are really 'into films,' as they say—I don't like that expression—is that films become their life. I think that's the worst thing for a filmmaker. If you can be interested in anything else, you will find that it will make you a live person, it will give you contact with what's going on, it will give you inspiration. If you sort of chase your tail and you go to films and you make films and you look at television and you talk to filmmakers, you will really lose. As a person, not just as a filmmaker."

FRANÇOIS TRUFFAUT, director

"Filmlovers are sick people. One goes into a movie house to seek a sense of security. One looks for something that is better organized than the world in which we live, and if one goes back to see the same film over and over, it's to be in a world where you can predict everything that is going to happen. I don't know if once one becomes a director one is cured."

MILTON KATSELAS, director and teacher

"Hitchcock said that the student director should not touch a camera for two years. The camera is a tool to express the story visually, but it should not be a substitute for handling the story. The first thing we must do in a film school is bring in actors and let these directors work with actors, so that we can see the problems they have. Give him a critique and let him work again with those actors and come back with a better scene. What this would do for the film director, first of all, would be to give him communication with the actor. He would not walk on a set with fear of the actor, concerned about what to say to the actor. There are some film directors who literally can't open their mouths to an actor. It's the same way Joe McCarthy felt about Communists: the enemy.

"A director always feels that unless he has the answers he's going to be in trouble. One of my first teachers was Elia Kazan, who said, 'Let them know you don't know. If there's a problem, then communicate straight with the actor and tell him, "I don't know the solution."' That's how you build confidence with an actor: you communicate with him. If, through your ideas, through your imagination, through your communication, through your conviction, you elicit the cooperation and agreement of your actors—not through enforcement—they will come on your side. And when they come on your side there is nothing that can stop you. If they are not on your side and are doing it under duress, then you're going to have troubles.

"Now, student directors will balk at this because the thing they really want to do is direct film. They want to get in back of that camera and start setting up the shots. They don't know what you mean when you say to them, 'You haven't made the moment.' They try to make the moment with a sudden cut or a close-up or a camera move, which is great, but the moment must also be made by the actor, and that moment can be made without a camera. By 'without a camera' I mean without a camera movement. You watch the work of Renoir and you find that there are incredible moments that occur and the camera doesn't move. The camera is still, and the camera is at a distance, much the same as you are in a theater. The longer you can keep the new director away from the camera, the better off you are."

JEANNE MOREAU, actress

"As an actress, you're different every time you work with a different director. The only way I prepare myself for a film and a director is to be empty. I do not have any idea in advance; I am ready to be filled up. I think that an actor or an actress is a medium, ready to take anything that passes by: indifference, coldness, aggression, warmth, love, hatred. Because sometimes you're hated. You don't know why. It's as though the director had to carry very violent emotions, and he takes them out on the people who are at his disposal, the people on the set. And it works, in a very strange way.

"Very good directors allow you a certain freedom once they have spoken with you; it gives you the sensation that you are your own director. Sometimes you give him what he wants plus something. Sometimes you give him less than he wants but you give him something else. You're trying to reach the director. He's your closest relationship, and though you don't look at him you feel his presence and his magnetism and his eyes. That's why no audience is needed. It's a very egotistic pleasure; it's really like lovemaking."

GILBERT CATES, director

"To me the most deplorable quality of most of the young actors I meet is the lack of humanities, their ignorance of the world, of history. It's the fact that they can't even spell Aeschylus, let alone have ever read a play of his. They regard Shakespeare as something their grandfathers once mentioned to them. There is such a dismal lack of interest. There is a narrowness of vision that allows a person to say, 'Well, OK, the play calls for a twenty-two-year-old surfer. I look like a twenty-two-year-old surfer. What do I have to know?'

"I think the best training for an actor at a certain age is not to study acting. The best training for an actor is to study the humanities, to study literature, to study history, to travel, to get a sense of who he is and what his relationship is to his environment and his relationship to his time. That's the passion he should develop. Then you learn the craft and, God willing, you have the craft and you have an understanding of yourself and the times in which you live. Then you can be an actor.

"One of the most extraordinary evenings I've spent was with Sir Laurence Olivier. It was fascinating talking to him because his conversation was not about acting; it was about England and the decline of the government, the decline of the country, its relationship to America, the power of politics—things that have nothing to do with acting and reading *Variety* and *Hollywood Reporter* and all the things most young actors regard as more important than anything else. So what I am saying is that the development of the person precedes the craft."

LEE GARMES, cinematographer

"I think the actors are more important than anything else. So I light the actors, and then I light the set. The actors, to me, are more important than the set. The set is only a background for you. It's like a sheet of paper to write on; the figures are what is important, not the paper."

GEORGE CUKOR, director

"If you have a good script, I certainly don't think you should allow actors to say, 'This is good, this isn't.' On the few occasions I've said yes, it's been disaster. If they don't like the script, they shouldn't do the goddamn script. You must have some regard for it. You must respect the script as much as you respect anything.

"I'll tell you what Helen Hayes said. She said she was absolutely appalled when people would say, 'Well, I don't know, this doesn't feel good,' and they would change the words. Helen said when she had difficulty with words, she'd just go to her dressing room and do it and do it and do it until she thought it was right. There's no such thing as 'No, I can't.' That's a lot of crap, and I think there's too much of that."

FEDERICO FELLINI, director

"It's absolutely impossible to improvise. Making a movie is a mathematical operation. It is like sending a missile to the moon. Art is a scientific operation. What we usually call improvisation is, in my case, just having an ear and an eye to things that occur during the time we are making the picture. The history of four months, five months of shooting is not only the private story of the director making the picture, it is also a story of a trip, of mutual relationships, of love, of enemies, of vanity. Everything has to do with the picture you are making, because everything is happening under this kind of atmosphere; so I think I am helped from everything.

"To be strictly faithful to what you have written four or five months before is a little silly sometimes. If you see that the picture is suggesting something new, you have to be open to this kind of suggestion, because sometimes it is the *picture* that directs *you* when you work in an open and honest way. That is *not* improvisation, that is just being faithful to what you are doing."

ERNEST LEHMAN, screenwriter

"Almost everyone unconsciously feels he knows as much about writing as a writer. It would be unthinkable for a writer to tell a director how to direct or a producer how to produce or an actor how to act or a cinematographer how to light a scene. But it is not at all unthinkable for *anyone* to tell a writer how to write. It comes with the territory. That is bound to produce problems for you, unless you have a superlatively integrated psyche where you can take anything and always remember that it's the picture that counts. However, your ego, your sense of professionalism come into play, and screenwriters often notice a glaze coming into the eyes of the director and the producer when the script is finished, and you get the subtle feeling that they would not weep if you got hit by a truck. I am not exaggerating.

"Sometimes it gets to be an antagonistic relationship, to put it mildly. I think you have to understand that people feel threatened by the writer. It's very curious. He knows something they don't know: he knows how to write. That's a subtle, disturbing quality that he has. And some directors, without even knowing it, resent the writer in the same way that a comedian might resent the fact that he ain't funny without twelve guys writing the jokes. The director knows that the script he is carrying around on the set every day was written by someone, yet that's just not something that all directors can digest easily."

MEL BROOKS, actor-writer-director

"Writers! Do not discuss embryo ideas! When you have coffee, don't talk to other people in the business about your ideas until they are fully written and registered. Then you can talk about them. You will not get help. You'll get envy and you'll get stealing. Also, not only will they get stolen, but you will let the vapor of creation escape when you tell it. Be a little schizophrenic, talk to yourself through the paper. It's a good exercise, and sometimes it makes money for you."

GORE VIDAL, writer

"Ever since that dread moment when Al Jolson said, 'You ain't heard nothin' yet'—which I think is the most sinister line in all of world drama—it's been a writer's medium. But nobody ever knew this. The directors know it. Cecil B. DeMille, that gorgeous egomaniac, said, 'You know, it's all the script.' Kurosawa said, 'It's the script.' I think even Delmer Daves would say it's the script. The script is all-important. But the director has got to get it away from the writer because he must be an *auteur du cinéma*.

"Almost anybody can do what a director does. I've worked on about fifteen movies; I've done 150 live television plays; I've done eight plays on Broadway—I never saw a director yet who contributed anything. When I got to Cannes for *The Best Man*—I got the critics' award for the best script—there on this banner was the title in French and: *Un film de Franklin Schaffner*. Well, I just hit the ceiling. I mean, this was my play, my movie. I had helped put the thing together; I had hired Frank. *'Un film de Franklin Schaffner'*! That's when I first ran into the auteur theory, in 1964. The French are always wrong, remember that."

MARIO PUZO, writer

"What happens after you do a script is—taking the case of *Superman*—you have a conference with the producers. All the suggestions they make will be to incorporate scenes from a movie that has just come out and has been a big success. They'll say, 'Why don't we have ten sharks around Superman?' or 'Why don't we have Darth Vader come out with his magic sword and try and kill Superman?' It gets really tiresome to sit there and listen to that stuff. That's when you earn your money. The writer does what he can, but he doesn't really have much of a say. They just do anything they want. There may be seven people rewriting the script. If you take it seriously, you're going to be killed. Something like *The Godfather* you fight about. The other stuff, like *Earthquake* and *Superman*, I had terrific fights simply as a matter of professional pride. I fight, but I don't go into hysterics over it. Writing novels, *you're* the boss, *you're* the studio."

EDWARD ANHALT, screenwriter

"In the olden times the writer wrote the thing and disappeared into the night, and there was no collaboration at all. A lot of awfully good pictures were made that way. So I really don't think there are any rules. It's a personal thing. And some very good pictures have been made where the actors never talked to the director.

"It has often been said, and I think it's very important, that films take on some sort of entity of their own; they escalate into something that's outside what was written, and they get to have a life of their own. Frequently the actors become involved in the story to the point where they live that life; they live it to the point of inventing things, and frequently those inventions are marvelous. A good director takes advantage of the psychosis of the actor, which is to act."

KING VIDOR, director

"The difficulty with movies is that you're depending on a lot of other people. But as far as I'm concerned, there's one guy who can say 'yes' or 'no,' and say 'This is the way I see it': the director. The big job is to find out who you are and get your individuality on the screen. I can't stress that too much. Look at Hitchcock. Every Hitchcock picture has the mark of an individual about it. It's true of John Ford, Frank Capra, Howard Hawks, Truffaut, Bergman, Fellini. It was true of DeMille; I didn't like his pictures at all, but they had his stamp on them.

"It sometimes takes years to find out who you are and what you are, because we don't accept ourselves as distinct individuals. We're trained not to be individuals. When you're very young your parents always want you to pattern yourself after them. So there's a great resistance to saying, 'What do I believe in? How do I feel? How do I see this?'—and not be ashamed of it. This is the number-one thing I've learned, to find out who you are and respect yourself, the divinity of yourself. If God isn't expressed by the individual, where the hell is He expressed? You have to be ingenious enough, have the guts, the courage, the determination to put yourself into whatever you're doing. Remember that, will you?"

PAUL MAZURSKY, writer-director

"I wrote *Harry and Tonto* with Josh Greenfield in 1971. And it was then turned down twenty-four times. It was an interesting experience because it has to do with 'What do they know? Are they right? Are they wrong? How do you keep going?' There were a lot of funny things that happened. I said, 'If the cat [Tonto, the companion of Art Carney in the film] is filled with coke and being smuggled cross-country, will you buy the picture?' I said it facetiously, and I got some 'yes' answers. But the point was that it will get made, if you really, really, *really* want to do it.

"I don't agree with a lot of people who put Hollywood down for the crap that's made. For the most part I think it's the obligation of the filmmaker. A lot of people just don't really want to make great films, and so they blame the system. The system is what it is. It's money and commerce. And every year there are a few fine films made. They get made because somebody really wanted to make them."

FRANK CAPRA, director

"If you follow trends you'll go broke faster than anybody in the world. If you start a trend, that's something else; but always go against the grain, never go with a trend. The trend, first of all, is morally wrong. You're trying to capitalize on something somebody else created, and it's dishonest to turn out carbon copies like that. You're not creating anything, you're just trying to make a fast buck on somebody else's creativity. You think that's what the audiences want, but the audiences don't know what they want. They only know when they see it, and they either love it or don't like it.

"People can't be programmed. I don't give a damn how many public-relations people there are in the world who say to you how many Nabiscos people are going to eat next year; they can't tell you. You cannot program the human spirit—impossible—and you cannot predict the human spirit. All you can hope is that what appeals to you will appeal to somebody else. Do what *you* want to do."

NICHOLAS MEYER, writer-director

"They're not conspicuous for brains, studio executives. With very few exceptions, they know nothing about storytelling, they know nothing about film. They're former agents; they make deals. They're not Jack Warner and Louis B. Mayer, semiliterate people who responded to tales. They don't know from that. They are taught like Benedictines to distrust the heart as deceitful above all things, and on no account to be swayed by personal opinion. They see that the W. C. Fields poster sells a lot, so they think, 'I don't give a shit about W. C. Fields, but the kids love it, so let's make a movie about W. C. Fields.' It's that kind of logic. You would not tell me a joke that you didn't think was funny on the off-chance that I might like it. Nobody does that, but that's the way they make movies."

MARTIN SCORSESE, director

"Roger Corman [head of New World Pictures] was the first person I brought *Mean Streets* to. Roger said, 'Marty, I understand we got a script from you, and everybody here says it's one of the best scripts we've received. However, I'd like to ask you one thing. I haven't read it. Has it got gangsters?' I said, 'Yes, it's got gangsters.' He said, 'Has it got guns?' I said, 'Yes, it's got guns.' He said, 'Has it got violence? Has it got sex?' I said, 'Yes.' He said, 'My brother Gene just made a picture called *Cool Breeze*. It's making a lot of money. Now, if you're willing to swing a little, I can give you $150,000 and you can shoot it all with a nonunion student crew in New York. The only thing is, I'd like the picture to be black.' Goes to show you how much I wanted to make the picture, I said, 'I'll think about it.' "

LEO GREENFIELD, studio executive

"I don't think any distribution-production company has a sense of social responsibility. This is a business for profit. You can't have a conscience. Otherwise you can't make certain films that make money. What were we [Warner Brothers] worried about in *The Exorcist*? That the Church would object. Why were we worried about the Church? Because we were worried about the Church per se? No. Because if the Church objected, it might hinder the impact of the film; consequently there would be a lesser gross. But who has really got a social conscience when they create? Think about it. Ringling Brothers sells something. We're selling something."

FRITZ LANG, director

"Have you seen *Deep Throat*? I am opposed to this film for a very simple reason. First of all, it is not film as art. But there's something else. If two young people, a boy and a girl, go in together, what they do when they are alone is their business, right? So one day they may find out there's another way to make love to each other. I go down on you and you go down on me, whatever you want. Something that is very beautiful for them if they find it out by themselves, if it comes out of their passion for each other. But they come and see it for the first time in a motion picture and say, 'Oh, let's try that.' For me, the whole thing is a crime against youth."

HASKELL WEXLER, cinematographer

"Directors can be directors and know less than any other person on the set. I'm really being serious. You can be a lousy cameraman or a cameraman who can't light too well but you have to know certain things. You have to know lenses, you have to know how to read a light meter, you have to know emulsions. There is a certain body of technical knowledge. If you're going to be a makeup man, there's a certain body of technical knowledge. If you're going to be a script clerk, there's a big body of technical knowledge. It is possible to be called a director in modern-day filmmaking and not know anything, except maybe the producer."

DAVID PUTTNAM, producer

"I hate corporations; therefore, I expect no form of morality from corporations. I expect morality from individuals. And that's why it's much more interesting for me to come and talk with you than go and talk to the board of Universal Pictures. I don't expect anything from them other than what they feel is required to keep their stock at the level they find acceptable. I do expect an awful lot of all of you in this room. Because you are individuals. And besides making a living, if your name's going to be on the screen, you've got to live with your conscience. You can change things. Without you, they don't exist. Always remember that: corporations don't exist without people. Somehow they've managed to perpetrate a terrific confidence trick. You have been convinced that you need them. In the end they need you; and the more gifted among you, they need desperately."

FRANK McCARTHY, producer

"If the top people in the studio will let you alone, and if you accept the full responsibility, then you must exercise the full authority. This doesn't mean that you strut around like Hitler, telling everyone what to do. It means that you try to develop relationships with the people *you* have selected to surround yourself with:

the director, the cutter, the cast, and all the rest. It is the function of the producer to realize his dream: to have a vision of what he wants to do, to know well in advance what he wants it to look like on the screen, and to follow through in the best way he can, without being a dictator, to realize that dream.

"Before you employ the director you must be sure he is somebody you can communicate with, and you must be sure that his vision of it is somewhat the same as yours—not in every detail, but somewhat the same. In other words, your *goals* are the same. The producer has to be responsible for the work, but he also has to give the director tremendous latitude, because the director is the most creative man on the film."

VILMOS ZSIGMOND, cinematographer

"The art director is very important. I wish all films would have good art directors. Laszlo Kovacs and I shot about seven pictures with the same art director, Leon Erickson, who did *McCabe and Mrs. Miller, Images, Cinderella Liberty*. You cannot always tell what his contribution is to a film, because you would credit the cameraman for certain moods, color or lighting effects, but we really have to pass some of the credit over to the art director. Many times you walk onto a set and everything is there; all you have to do is turn on a couple lights. If you start out with a good set, obviously you are already inspired. You can perfect your lighting and then you have great mood. On *McCabe and Mrs. Miller*, it was a ball to work on those sets. Everything looked just right, the kerosene lamps he brought in—it was a joy to work on sets which were perfect."

VICTOR J. KEMPER, cinematographer

"The directors who are the most fun to work with are the ones who are the most prepared. This is as opposed to the directors who come in and improvise, which is the case more often than not: everybody sits around and waits, the crews all splinter off, there's a card game over here, and they're shooting craps in that corner.

"There are two kinds of prepared directors. One is the director who is prepared in terms of his actors and the script; he can convey to you very easily what he wants out of the scene in terms of moods, passions, whatever. That leaves you free to establish a look with lenses and shots. And then there's the other director who is just as good visually as he is with actors, even to the point of having storyboards drawn. That's also fine, because it isn't easy to take someone else's preconceived notion and make it work exactly the way he wanted it to work.

"Some cameramen have said, 'No director is going to tell me how to shoot my movie.' Well, you all have to know that is nonsense, because every movie is the director's movie. It's true that the producer puts up the money, but it is the director who really decides what that movie is going to be on the screen. The best thing a good cameraman can do is give the director exactly what he expects."

ROMAN POLANSKI, director

"A good cameraman can function only with a good director. It is very difficult to do good photography with a lousy director."

RICHARD ATTENBOROUGH, actor-director

"I don't have to tell you, cinema is the director's medium beyond all others. If you're directing, you have the opportunity to put your signature on the bottom of the frame. You have the opportunity to say, 'That is what I believe.'

"I come from a very radical family. My sympathies are very much to the left, and I have certain *cris de coeur* and credos which I wish to state. I wish to make a plea to the strong for the weak. I wish to persuade those to whom power is important and authority is important that a display of tolerance and compassion is not, in fact, a display of weakness but, indeed, a display of even greater strength. I wish to make pleas for all sorts of causes.

"The cinema permits me to do this. And if I am granted the opportunity of being able to direct a picture of which I have total control, then my opportunity—in a medium which is the most widespread communication medium that we've yet devised—is heaven-sent, God-sent. To have that chance, to be able to make those statements, is the sort of thing anybody prays for. Therefore, I would wish to direct."

DAVID LEAN, director

"I must tell you, I find it all terribly difficult when I'm shooting a film. About twice a week, I'm absolutely stuck and don't know how to do it. I'm sitting here like some wise old bird. I'm not. What is directing? It's trying to use a lot of people and some very, very heavy apparatus and give it the lightness of a pen while you are writing."

SYDNEY POLLACK, director

"If somebody asked me what is the most important thing about directing, I would say to be in good physical shape. I'm now forty-three years old, which is not old, but I'm not a kid either. And the difference between how I feel now and how I felt ten years ago is enormous. For the first time in my life, I have begun to understand directors I thought were crazy when they would say 'I'm too old to do this film. Get a younger director.' The fact of the matter is that it's the most enormously grueling physical exercise you can go through, partly because there is so much emotional strain.

"It's not just a question of can you solve the artistic problem —for every moment that it takes you to solve the artistic problem, it's costing millions of dollars. And millions of dollars makes people behave badly. Grown men behave like five-year-olds. They cry. They threaten you. They get hysterical. Actors, who have careers at stake and believe that you are going to destroy their careers, will get crazy at three in the morning and call you, and fight with each other, and won't come out of the trailer, and so on. Everybody comes to you every minute with a decision.

"What you do is put yourself in a certain gear, like you put a car in gear. You have to. You don't permit yourself to give in to the anxiety. Plus the fact that they're all looking to you as the strong one, you know? If you start to get crazy it's very bad. So you pace yourself. I train between pictures, as hard as I can, but usually, by the time I finish a picture, I'm in horrible shape. Christ Almighty, in a picture you drink, you smoke four packs of cigarettes a day, you don't even know you're lighting them. You light a cigarette every time you say 'Cut!' and the minute you say 'Roll it' you throw one out. You light the wrong end, you stick them in your ear, you just get crazy.

"You start at six A.M. and you're wired all day. If you produce your own pictures, then after you see the dailies at seven P.M. and you finish at eight, you go into a production meeting at eight-thirty about how much over budget you are. The trucks are costing money, and they won't give you permission to shoot on the street the day after tomorrow. If you don't do it, you're $2 million over the budget. You finish that at eleven P.M. Then you have to eat before you can go to bed. So the first thing you reach for is a glass of Scotch, and before you know it, you've creamed half of a bottle. You fall into bed. You wake up in the morning hung over and you drink fifteen cups of coffee.

"I don't believe I'm exaggerating one bit, and I believe that if you got any director here to tell you the honest-to-God truth, they would tell you the same thing. Anybody who tells you that he isn't scared to death directing a $10-million movie with major stars is a liar. It just can't be done. I don't care if you're a hundred years old, you're still scared, because you've got a reputation at stake. You say, 'Jesus Christ, if this one isn't as good as the last one, then I've failed.' And there's this constant anxiety between trying to get what you want, and technical problems, and a producer who's yelling at you. In every picture there is one of those scenes where you just say, 'God, I don't know how I'm going to do this scene.' And then you start working your way through it.

"Now, I say what I've just said to you, and yet, if you ever came on a set where I'm working, you would say, 'Jeez, you're so calm, so unruffled. You never yell. You handle it so easily.' But they don't know what's going on inside. You just get very adept in the art of hiding whatever anxiety you have."

ELIA KAZAN, writer-director

"The greatest loss you people have out here in Hollywood is that there are fewer stimuli between the place where you live and the place where you work. I'm a fellow who gets a lot from what he sees around. In New York City I live on 68th Street and I write in a little office on 54th Street; there are always five, ten, fifteen things I see on the walk down that I can't forget. The other day I was riding the train to visit my mother in Rye, and there was a girl on the train with a Vivaldi concerto open in her lap, a rather plain little twelve-year-old girl with a little sweet face, and she was playing an imaginary piano.

"I began to think, where would I possibly see that in Los Angeles? You could never see this here because no one rides a train. I never see a goddamned thing. I get up in the morning; my wife gives me breakfast; I get in the car that the studio provides; I ride down Beverly Boulevard and go to Paramount Studios. I ride semiconsciously; I don't see anything because I'm thinking about what I'm going to do. I get to the studio and I'm in an office, which is a protected environment; the secretary is just outside the door and she's doing what I tell her. That goes on all the time and that's all. I feel terribly isolated here; I feel denatured here."

PAUL MAZURSKY, writer-director

"You know, it's strange. If you live in this town and you go to the supermarket, the box boy says, 'I've got a fabulous script.' If you go to the gas station, the guy at the pump is an actor, probably. The only ones I have met who aren't in the business are the ones in the business."

MIKE MEDAVOY, studio executive

"There is a relatively small talent pool. As an agent I used to have a saying, which was that there are two hundred people in the whole business, and since I was on the phone with fifty of them a day, sometime during the week I would talk to all two hundred. And you could play a game called 'telephone': you start a rumor on Monday morning and see how it comes back on Friday, because it will come back quite differently. The fact is, we need to expand that pool, we need talent, we need people who will go out and make movies."

MICHAEL CRICHTON, writer-director

"Everyone will give you a different idea, but my idea is that what counts is persistence. The movie business is a business which traditionally many people have wanted to get into. Who gets to do it when a lot of people want to do it? The people who want it most badly. Some people are like a rat trying to get into the kitchen where they know the cheese is. They keep going through different alleyways and finally they find the soft spot and chew their way through. That's how it works. It's individual. I don't believe that anybody helps anybody else, really. You just do it yourself. You find some way."

SHERRY LANSING, studio executive

"There has been a long period of time when there were enormously talented women and the doors were not open to them in executive positions, or in any positions. Once the walls start to be broken down, then it becomes natural to hire the best person for the job, be that a man or a woman. When we have true equality you won't say 'There are more women being hired now.' It will just be natural. The important thing is that we get to a point where it is simply that you are judged on your qualifications for the job, period."

JOAN MICKLIN SILVER, director

"I had such blatantly sexist things said to me by studio executives when I started, the most outstanding of which was: 'Feature films are very expensive to mount and to distribute, and woman directors are one more problem we don't need.' I don't think there's a single executive who would say that to a woman director today [1979]. He might think it, but nobody would say it, so we're that step ahead. Three women have made films for studios this year. That's a lot more than any other year since the silent-film era: Anne Bancroft and Nancy Walker and I. On the other hand, half the people in the world are women, so why wouldn't half the directors of movies be women? So, long way to go."

ROBERT ALDRICH, director

"It's not a matter of 'Can you?' It's who is going to let you. You see people who probably could be marvelous directors if somebody would say, 'You start tomorrow.' It really has so little to do with qualification and so much to do with luck that you're very reluctant to tell young people that the harder they work the more chances there are for them to get a start. It really is not true. You see dummies get opportunities who don't deserve it. Then you see people who are entitled to a shot and they don't get it. I don't pretend to know the answer to that."

ALBERT S. RUDDY, producer

"You've got to be neurotic, insane, or totally obsessed to make it in this business. What other business demands that you gamble the most important thing that you have in your life: your time? When you're young, that time is crucial, because if you don't make it at a certain point, you're not going to work as a junior executive at General Motors. Along that way, your chances of what we call a normal life are also very difficult, because of your anxiety, worrying about whether you are going to make it. You don't have any money, there's very little opportunity to start working, so you must sustain that fantasy you have. And this is the most horrendous part of it—even if you're willing to suffer the anxieties, even if you're willing to give up the things other people want, the chances of making it are still one in a thousand. You wouldn't play odds like that in Las Vegas, would you?

"To make it requires no genius. There are no secrets. It's how much you work. There's no one in this room who can't do it if you want it. Most people drift out because they can't make it. Fifty percent of this group will not be interested in doing this three or four years from today. Of course, the other 50 percent will have fun!"

WILLIAM WYLER, director

"I have a theory: it is not to bore the audience. That's a good theory. It sometimes seems like all the damn pictures are too long, mine included. Some of the directors don't seem to give a damn about anything except their own feelings. There's a very fine line between self-confidence and arrogance. It's fine to have self-confidence—in a way you make pictures for yourself, but you also make them for an audience. Especially if you make a film that has something to say. If you want to convey that thought to a large audience, then you must make them accept it and like it. Otherwise, if you just say it to a handful of people, you have not succeeded in getting your message across."

RICHARD BROOKS, writer-director

"If you want to be in movies, you'd better love them a lot, because it's going to break your heart. When you've finished the picture and the studio sees it for the first time they will break your heart, because they'll say that four minutes and thirty-one seconds ought to be taken out of there, and you'll say, 'Why four minutes and thirty-one seconds?' 'Well, I don't know. I just have a feel.' They're full of shit. They'd just like to get one more showing a day. So they'll break your heart. And when the picture opens maybe the audience will break your heart. Statistics alone will tell you that 60 or 70 percent of the time you're going to fail. By 'fail'

I mean that it won't make money. And most of the time the critics today are reviewing each other; you're caught somewhere in the middle, and you don't understand what the hell they mean, so *they're* going to break your heart.

"It's going to be rough on you. But if you love it and your real reward is *in the making* of the picture, not in getting in that big fucking black limousine and going out there for opening night where they take all the pictures and they've got the big dinner afterward and all that crap—your reward is that *when that picture is finished you've already been paid.* That's where your payoff is— in the making of it, from the very beginning to the end."

WILLIAM BOWERS, screenwriter

"I want to tell you one more story and then we'll call it off. I did a picture called *Night and Day*, which was the life of Cole Porter. Cary Grant had me brought in. They had been working on the script for two years. They were due to start shooting the next week, and they decide they can't use anything in the script. Now there is a marvelous Hungarian by the name of Mike Curtiz directing it, and I go in for the first meeting with him and he says, 'You know this Cole Porter?' I say, 'No, I don't know him, but I know who he is.' 'I'm going to tell you about him,' he says. 'When he was born he was given $6 million for being born. And when he was twelve years old he was given $10 million just for being twelve years old. He goes to Yale University. He meets this girl, they get married, and she is worth $20 million. He goes out and he writes all these goddamn songs and makes another $8 million. I figure what we've got in this story is a case of struggle, struggle, struggle.' It was a ghastly picture, too."

Suggested Reading

These listings include books on the seminar participants and their work, and other books of interest dealing with the general areas of filmmaking in which the participants are involved.

THE STUDIO EXECUTIVE

McClintick, David. *Indecent Exposure: A True Story of Hollywood and Wall Street.* New York: Morrow, 1982.

Marx, Samuel. *Mayer and Thalberg: The Make-Believe Saints.* New York: Random House, 1975.

Ross, Lillian. *Picture.* New York: Rinehart, 1952.

Thomas, Bob. *King Cohn.* New York: Putnam, 1963.

Thomas, Bob. *Thalberg: Life and Legend.* New York: Doubleday, 1969.

Wallis, Hal, and Charles Higham. *Starmaker: The Autobiography of Hal Wallis.* New York: Macmillan, 1980.

Warner, Jack L., with Dean Jennings. *My First Hundred Years in Hollywood.* New York: Random House, 1964.

Zukor, Adolph. *The Public Is Never Wrong.* New York: Putnam, 1953.

THE PRODUCER

Dunne, John Gregory. *The Studio.* New York: Farrar, Straus & Giroux, 1969.

Fowler, Gene. *Father Goose: The Story of Mack Sennett.* New York: Covici, Friede, 1934.

Gottlieb, Carl. *The "Jaws" Log.* New York: Dell, 1975.

Gussow, Mel. *Don't Say Yes Until I Finish Talking: A Biography of Darryl F. Zanuck.* New York: Doubleday, 1971.

Kanin, Garson. *Hollywood.* New York: Viking, 1974.

Korda, Michael. *Charmed Lives: A Family Romance.* New York: Random House, 1979.

Selznick, David O., edited by Rudy Behlmer. *Memo from David O. Selznick.* New York: Viking, 1972.

Thomas, Bob. *Walt Disney.* New York: Simon and Schuster, 1976.

THE DIRECTOR

Bergman, Ingmar. *Four Screenplays of Ingmar Bergman [Smiles of a Summer Night, The Seventh Seal, Wild Strawberries, and The Magician].* Translated by Lars Malstrom and David Kushner. New York: Simon and Schuster, 1960.

Bergman, Ingmar, interviewed by Stig Björkman, Torsten Manns, and Jonas Sima. *Bergman on Bergman.* Translated by Paul Britten Austin. New York: Simon and Schuster, 1973.

Capra, Frank. *The Name Above the Title.* New York: Macmillan, 1971.

Kaminsky, Stuart M. (editor), with Joseph F. Hill. *Ingmar Bergman: Essays in Criticism.* New York: Oxford University Press, 1975.

Sarris, Andrew. *The American Cinema.* New York: Dutton, 1969.

Sherman, Eric (editor), for The American Film Institute. *Directing the Film: Film Directors on Their Art.* Boston: Little, Brown, 1976.

Truffaut, François, with Helen G. Scott. *Hitchcock.* New York: Simon and Schuster, 1966.

Wood, Robin. *Ingmar Bergman.* New York: Praeger, 1969.

THE SCREENWRITER

Brady, John. *The Craft of the Screenwriter.* New York: Simon and Schuster, 1981.

Corliss, Richard (editor). *The Hollywood Screenwriters.* New York: Avon, 1972.

Corliss, Richard. *Talking Pictures: Screenwriters in the American Cinema, 1927–1973.* Woodstock, N.Y.: Overlook Press, 1974.

Dardis, Tom. *Some Time in the Sun.* New York: Scribner, 1976.

Froug, William. *The Screenwriter Looks at the Screenwriter.* New York: Macmillan, 1972.

Hecht, Ben. *A Child of the Century.* New York: Simon and Schuster, 1954.

Wilder, Billy, and I.A.L. Diamond. *Some Like It Hot.* New York: New American Library, 1959.

Wilder, Billy, and I.A.L. Diamond. *The Apartment and The Fortune Cookie: Two Screenplays.* New York: Praeger, 1971.

Zolotow, Maurice. *Billy Wilder in Hollywood.* New York: Putnam, 1977.

THE ACTOR

Cripps, Thomas. *Slow Fade to Black: The Negro in American Film, 1900–1942.* New York: Oxford University Press, 1977.

Cripps, Thomas. *Black Film as Genre.* Bloomington: Indiana University Press, 1978.

The Editors of *Freedomways. Paul Robeson: The Great Forerunner.* New York: Dodd, Mead, 1978.

Hoffman, William. *Sidney.* New York: Lyle Stuart, 1971.

Keyser, Lester J., and André H. Ruszkowski. *The Cinema of Sidney Poitier.* Cranbury, N.J.: A.S. Barnes, 1980.

Leab, Daniel J. *From Sambo to Superspade: The Black Experience in Motion Pictures.* Boston: Houghton Mifflin, 1975.

Poitier, Sidney. *This Life.* New York: Knopf, 1980.

Ross, Lillian, and Helen Ross. *The Player: A Profile of an Art.* New York: Simon and Schuster, 1962.

THE ACTRESS

Andrews, Bart. *Lucy & Ricky & Fred & Ethel: The Story of "I Love Lucy."* New York: Dutton, 1976.

Andrews, Bart, and Thomas J. Watson. *Loving Lucy: An Illustrated Tribute to Lucille Ball.* New York: St. Martin's, 1980.

Blesh, Rudi. *Keaton.* New York: Macmillan, 1966.

Durgnat, Raymond. *The Crazy Mirror: Hollywood Comedy and the American Image.* London: Faber and Faber, 1969.

Epstein, Edward Z., and Joe Morella. *Lucy: The Bittersweet Life of Lucille Ball.* Secaucus, N.J.: Lyle Stuart, 1973.

Haskell, Molly. *From Reverence to Rape: The Treatment of Women in the Movies.* New York: Holt, Rinehart & Winston, 1973.

Kay, Karyn, and Gerald Peary (editors). *Women and the Cinema.* New York: Dutton, 1977.

THE CINEMATOGRAPHER

Balshofer, Fred J., and Arthur C. Miller, with the assistance of Bebe Bergsten. *One Reel a Week.* Berkeley: University of California Press, 1967.

Brownlow, Kevin. *The Parade's Gone By.* New York: Knopf, 1968.

Campbell, Russell (compiler and editor). *Practical Motion Picture Photography.* Cranbury, N.J.: A.S. Barnes, 1970.

Higham, Charles. *Hollywood Cameramen: Sources of Light.* Bloomington: Indiana University Press, 1970.

Maltin, Leonard. *The Art of the Cinematographer.* New York: Dover, 1978.

Rainsberger, Todd. *James Wong Howe, Cinematographer.* Cranbury, N.J.: A.S. Barnes, 1981.

Young, Freddie, and Paul Petzold. *The Work of the Motion Picture Cameraman.* New York: Hastings House, 1972.

THE COMPOSER

Bazelon, Irwin. *Knowing the Score: Notes on Film Music.* New York: Van Nostrand, 1975.

Eisenstein, Sergei. *The Film Form.* New York: Harcourt, Brace, 1949.

Eisenstein, Sergei. *The Film Sense.* New York: Harcourt, Brace, 1947.

Evans, Mark. *Soundtrack: The Music of the Movies.* New York: Hopkinson & Blake, 1975.

Huntley, John, and Roger Manvell. *The Technique of Film Music*. New York: Hastings House, 1957 *et seq*.

Limbacher, James L. (editor). *Film Music: From Violin to Video*. Metuchen, N.J.: Scarecrow Press, 1974.

Prendergast, Roy M. *Film Music: A Neglected Art*. New York: Norton, 1977.

Thomas, Tony. *Music for the Movies*. Cranbury, N.J.: A.S. Barnes, 1973.

THE PRODUCTION DESIGNER

Barsacq, Léon, revised and edited by Elliott Stein. *Caligari's Cabinet and Other Grand Illusions: A History of Film Design*. Boston: New York Graphic Society, 1976.

Chase, Donald (editor), for The American Film Institute. *Filmmaking: The Collaborative Art*. Boston: Little, Brown, 1975.

Corliss, Mary, and Carlos Clarens (assemblers), "The Hollywood Art Director." Special section of *Film Comment* magazine, May–June 1978.

Larson, Orville K. (editor). *Scene Design for Stage and Screen*. East Lansing: Michigan State University Press, 1961.

Marner, Terence St. John. *Film Design*. Cranbury, N.J.: A.S. Barnes, 1974.

THE EDITOR

Crittenden, Roger. *The Thames and Hudson Manual of Film Editing*. London: Thames and Hudson, 1981.

Nizhny, Vladimir. *Lessons with Eisenstein*. Translated by Ivor Montagu and Jay Leyda. London: George Allen and Unwin, 1962.

Reisz, Karel, and Gavin Millar. *The Technique of Film Editing*. New York: Hastings House, 1953 *et seq*.

Rosenblum, Ralph, and Robert Karen. *When the Shooting Stops . . . the Cutting Begins*. New York: Viking, 1979.

THE COSTUME DESIGNER

Chierichietti, David. *Hollywood Costume Design.* New York: Harmony Books, 1976.

McConathy, Dale, with Diana Vreeland. *Hollywood Costume.* New York: Harry N. Abrams, in cooperation with the Metropolitan Museum of Art, 1976.

THE AGENT

Brenner, Marie. *Going Hollywood: An Insider's Look at Power and Pretense in the Movie Business.* New York: Delacorte, 1978.

Kohner, Frederick. *The Magician of Sunset Boulevard: The Improbable Life of Paul Kohner, Hollywood Agent.* Palos Verdes, Calif.: Morgan Press, 1977.

Index

207

About the Editor

Joseph McBride is an author and screenwriter whose scripts include the cult classic *Rock 'n' Roll High School* and several television specials, including the American Film Institute Life Achievement Award tributes to James Stewart, Fred Astaire, Frank Capra, and John Huston, for which he has received an Emmy nomination and three Writers Guild of America Awards nominations. He has written or edited twelve other books, including *John Ford, Orson Welles, Hawks on Hawks,* and *High & Inside: The Complete Guide to Baseball Slang.* He was formerly business editor and film critic for *Variety* and *Daily Variety.*